Quick & Easy
Pasta

p

Contents

Introduction

Pasta has existed in one form or another since the days of the Roman Empire and remains one of the most versatile ingredients in the kitchen. It can be combined with almost anything from meat to fish, vegetables to fruit, and is even delicious served with simple herb sauces. No pantry should be without a supply of dried pasta, which, combined with a few other stock ingredients, can be turned into a mouthwatering and nutritious meal within minutes.

Why eat pasta?

Most pasta is made from durum wheat flour and contains protein and carbohydrates. It is a good source of slow-release energy and has the additional advantage of being value for money.

Varieties

There is an enormous range of different types of pasta, some of which are listed on the opposite page. Many are available both dried and fresh. Unless you have access to a good Italian delicatessen, it is probably not worth buying fresh, unfilled pasta, but even large stores sell high-quality tortellini, capelletti, ravioli, and agnolotti. Best of all is to make fresh pasta at home. It takes a little time, but is quite easy and well worth the effort. You can mix the dough by hand or prepare it in a food processor if you prefer.

Colors and flavors

Pasta may be colored and flavored with extra ingredients that are usually added with the beaten egg:
Black: add 1 tsp squid or cuttlefish ink.
Green: add 4 oz/115 g well-drained cooked spinach when kneading.
Purple: work 1 large, cooked beet in a food processor and add with an extra ½ cup flour.
Red: add 2 tbsp tomato paste.

Cooking pasta

Always use a large pan for cooking pasta and bring lightly salted water to a boil. Add the pasta and 1 tbsp olive oil, but do not cover or the water will boil over. Quickly bring the water back to a rolling boil and avoid overcooking. When the pasta is tender, but still firm to the bite, drain and toss with butter, olive oil, or your prepared sauce, and serve as soon as possible.

The cooking times given here are guidelines only:

Fresh unfilled pasta: 2–3 minutes
Fresh filled pasta: 8–10 minutes
Dried unfilled pasta: 10–12 minutes
Dried filled pasta: 15–20 minutes

Basic Pasta Dough

If you wish to make your own pasta for the dishes in this book, follow this simple recipe.

SERVES 4

INGREDIENTS

4 cups durum wheat flour

4 eggs, lightly beaten

1 tbsp olive oil

salt

1 Lightly flour a counter. Sift the flour with a pinch of salt into a mound. Make a well in the center and add the eggs and olive oil.

2 Using a fork or your fingertips, gradually work the mixture until the ingredients are combined. Knead vigorously for 10–15 minutes.

3 Set the dough aside to rest for 25 minutes, before rolling it out as thinly and evenly as possible and using as desired.

Types of pasta

There are as many as 200 different pasta shapes and about three times as many names for them. New shapes are being designed—and named—all the time and the same shape may be called a different name in different regions of Italy.

anelli, anellini: *small rings for soup*

bucatini: *long, medium-thick tubes*

cannelloni: *large, thick, round pasta tubes*

capelli d'angelo: *thin strands of "angel hair"*

conchiglie: *ridged shells*

conchigliette: *little shells*

cresti di gallo: *curved-shaped*

ditali, ditalini: *short tubes*

eliche: *loose spirals*

farfalle: *bows*

fettuccine: *medium ribbons*

fusilli: *spirals*

gemelli: *two pieces wrapped together as "twins"*

lasagna: *flat, rectangular sheets*

linguine: *long, flat ribbons*

lumache: *snail-shaped shells*

lumaconi: *big shells*

macaroni: *long- or short-cut tubes*

orecchiette: *ear-shaped*

penne: *quill-shaped*

rigatoni: *thick, ridged tubes*

spaghetti: *fine or medium rods*

tagliarini: *thin ribbons*

tagliatelle: *broad ribbons*

vermicelli: *fine pasta, usually folded into skeins*

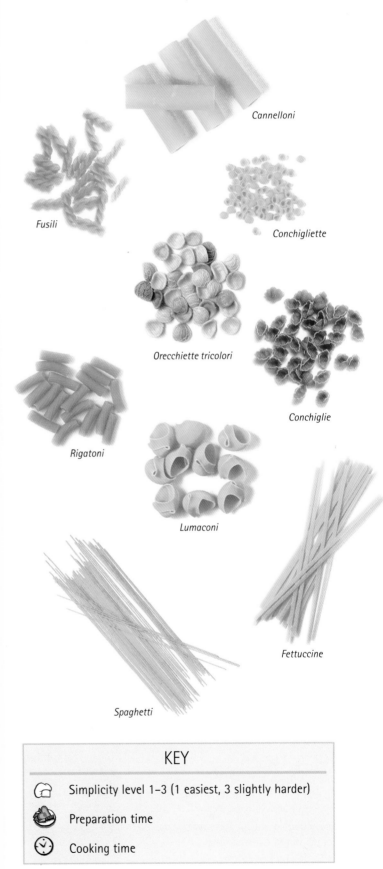

Cannelloni

Fusili

Conchigliette

Orecchiette tricolori

Conchiglie

Rigatoni

Lumaconi

Fettuccine

Spaghetti

KEY

🍳	Simplicity level 1–3 (1 easiest, 3 slightly harder)
🔔	Preparation time
🕐	Cooking time

Italian Cream of Tomato Soup

Plum tomatoes are ideal for making soups and sauces, as they have denser, less watery flesh than other varieties.

NUTRITIONAL INFORMATION

Calories	 555	Sugars	.... 18g
Protein	.... 11g	Fat	.... 32g
Carbohydrate	.. 60g	Saturates	..... 19g

🍖 15 mins   🕐 40 mins

SERVES 4

I N G R E D I E N T S

4 tbsp unsalted butter

1 large onion, chopped

2½ cups vegetable bouillon

2 lb/900 g Italian plum tomatoes, skinned and roughly chopped

pinch of baking soda

8 oz/225 g dried fusilli

1 tbsp superfine sugar

⅔ cup heavy cream

salt and pepper

fresh basil leaves, to garnish

deep-fried croûtons, to serve

1 Melt the butter in a large pan, add the onion and cook for 3 minutes. Add 1¼ cups of vegetable bouillon to the pan, with the chopped tomatoes and baking soda. Bring the soup to a boil and simmer for 20 minutes.

2 Remove the pan from the heat and set aside to cool. Purée the soup in a blender or food processor and pour through a fine strainer back into the pan, pushing it through with a wooden spoon.

3 Add the remaining vegetable bouillon and the fusilli to the pan, and season to taste with salt and pepper.

4 Add the sugar to the pan, bring to a boil, then lower the heat and simmer for about 15 minutes.

5 Pour the soup into a warm serving bowl, swirl the cream around the surface and garnish with fresh basil. Serve immediately with deep-fried croûtons.

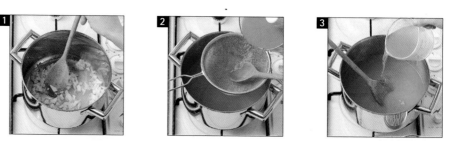

COOK'S TIP

To make tomato and carrot soup, add half the quantity again of vegetable bouillon with the same amount of carrot juice and 1¼ cups grated carrot to the recipe, cooking the carrot with the onion.

Lemon & Chicken Soup

This delicately flavored summer soup is surprisingly easy to make, and tastes absolutely delicious.

NUTRITIONAL INFORMATION

Calories	506	Sugars	4g
Protein	19g	Fat	31g
Carbohydrate	41g	Saturates	19g

🍲 🍲

🔥 5–10 mins   ⏱ 1¼ hrs

SERVES 4

I N G R E D I E N T S

4 tbsp butter

8 shallots, thinly sliced

2 carrots, thinly sliced

2 celery stalks, thinly sliced

8 oz/225 g boned chicken breasts, finely chopped

3 lemons

5 cups chicken bouillon

8 oz/225 g dried spaghetti, broken into small pieces

⅔ cup heavy cream

salt and white pepper

T O G A R N I S H

fresh parsley sprig

3 lemon slices, halved

1 Melt the butter in a large pan. Add the shallots, carrots, celery, and chicken and cook over a low heat, stirring occasionally, for 8 minutes.

2 Thinly pare the lemons and blanch the rind in boiling water for 3 minutes. Squeeze the juice from the lemons.

3 Add the lemon rind and juice and the chicken bouillon to the pan. Bring slowly to a boil over a low heat. Simmer for 40 minutes, stirring occasionally.

4 Add the spaghetti to the pan and cook for 15 minutes. Season to taste with salt and white pepper and add the cream. Heat through, but do not let the soup boil or it will curdle.

5 Pour the soup into a large serving bowl or individual soup bowls, garnish with the parsley and half slices of lemon, and serve immediately.

COOK'S TIP

You can prepare this soup up to the end of step 3 in advance, so that all you need do before serving is heat it through before adding the pasta and the finishing touches.

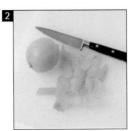
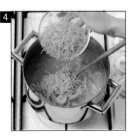

Chicken & Corn Soup

This warming, creamy chicken soup is made into a meal in itself with the addition of strands of vermicelli.

NUTRITIONAL INFORMATION

Calories	457	Sugars	3g
Protein	16g	Fat	21g
Carbohydrate	36g	Saturates	12g

5 mins   30 mins

SERVES 4

INGREDIENTS

1 lb/450 g boned chicken breasts, cut into strips

5 cups chicken bouillon

⅔ cup heavy cream

3½ oz/100 g dried vermicelli

1 tbsp cornstarch

3 tbsp milk

6 oz/175 g corn kernels

salt and pepper

1 Put the chicken, bouillon, and cream into a large pan and bring to a boil over a low heat. Reduce the heat slightly and simmer for about 20 minutes. Season the soup with salt and pepper to taste.

COOK'S TIP

If you are short of time, buy ready-cooked chicken, remove any skin and cut it into slices.

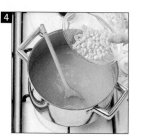

2 Meanwhile, cook the vermicelli in lightly salted boiling water for 10–12 minutes, or until just tender. Drain the pasta and keep warm.

3 In a small bowl, mix together the cornstarch and milk to make a smooth paste. Stir the cornstarch mixture into the soup until it has thickened.

4 Add the corn kernels and vermicelli to the pan and heat through.

5 Transfer the soup to a warm serving bowl or individual soup bowls and serve immediately.

Spaghetti alla Carbonara

Ensure that all of the cooked ingredients are as hot as possible before adding the eggs, so that they cook on contact.

NUTRITIONAL INFORMATION

Calories ..... 1092 Sugars 9g
Protein .... 37g Fat 69g
Carbohydrate .. 86g Saturates 36g

10 mins 5–10 mins

SERVES 4

I N G R E D I E N T S

15 oz/425 g dried spaghetti

2 tbsp olive oil

1 large onion, thinly sliced

2 garlic cloves, chopped

6 oz/175 g rindless bacon, cut into thin strips

2 tbsp butter

6 oz/175 g mushrooms, thinly sliced

1¼ cups heavy cream

3 eggs, beaten

1 cup freshly grated Parmesan cheese, plus extra to serve (optional)

salt and pepper

fresh sage sprigs, to garnish

1 Warm a large serving dish or bowl. Bring a large pan of lightly salted water to a boil. Add the spaghetti and 1 tablespoon of the oil and cook until tender, but still firm to the bite. Drain, return to the pan and keep warm.

2 Meanwhile, heat the remaining oil in a skillet over a medium heat. Add the onion and cook until it is transparent. Add the garlic and bacon and cook until the bacon is crisp. Transfer to the warm plate and keep warm.

3 Melt the butter in the skillet. Add the sliced mushrooms and cook, stirring occasionally, for 3–4 minutes. Return the bacon mixture to the pan. Cover and keep warm.

4 Mix together the cream, eggs, and cheese in a bowl and season to taste.

5 Working very quickly, tip the spaghetti into the bacon and mushroom mixture and pour over the beaten eggs. Toss the spaghetti quickly into the egg and cream mixture, using 2 forks. Garnish with sage and, if you wish, extra Parmesan. Serve immediately.

COOK'S TIP
The key to success with this recipe is not to overcook the egg. It is important to keep the ingredients hot enough just to cook the egg and to work rapidly to avoid scrambling it.

Spicy Chorizo Vermicelli

Simple and quick to make, this spicy dish will set the taste buds tingling, with its wild mushrooms, chiles, and anchovies.

NUTRITIONAL INFORMATION

Calories	672	Sugars	1g
Protein	16g	Fat	27g
Carbohydrate	90g	Saturates	6g

🍲 5 mins   🕐 10–12 mins

SERVES 6

I N G R E D I E N T S

1½ lb/680 g dried vermicelli

½ cup olive oil

2 garlic cloves

4½ oz/125 g chorizo, sliced

8 oz/225 g wild mushrooms

3 fresh red chiles, chopped

2 tbsp freshly grated Parmesan cheese

salt and pepper

anchovy fillets, to garnish

1 Bring a large pan of lightly salted water to a boil. Add the vermicelli and 1 tablespoon of the oil, and cook until just al dente—tender, but still firm to the bite. Drain, and place on a large, heated plate to keep warm.

2 Meanwhile heat the remaining oil in a large skillet. Add the garlic, and cook for 1 minute. Add the chorizo and wild mushrooms and cook for 4 minutes, then add the chopped chiles and cook for a minute more.

3 Pour the chorizo and wild mushroom mixture over the vermicelli, and season with a little salt and pepper. Sprinkle over freshly grated Parmesan cheese, garnish with a lattice of anchovy fillets, and serve the dish immediately.

VARIATION

Fresh sardines may be used in this recipe in place of the anchovies. However, ensure that you gut and clean the sardines, removing the backbone, before using them.

Tricolor Timballini

An unusual way of serving pasta, these cheese molds are excellent with a crunchy salad for a light lunch.

NUTRITIONAL INFORMATION

Calories	 529	Sugars	.... 7g
Protein	.... 18g	Fat	.... 29g
Carbohydrate	.. 46g	Saturates	..... 12g

🔥 🔥 🔥

🍲 30 mins   🕐 1 hr

SERVES 4

I N G R E D I E N T S

1 tbsp butter, softened

1 cup dried white breadcrumbs

6 oz/175 g dried tricolor spaghetti, broken into 2 inch/5 cm lengths

1 tbsp olive oil

1 egg yolk

1 cup grated Swiss cheese

1¼ cups Béchamel Sauce (see page 38)

tomato

TOMATO SAUCE

2 tbsp olive oil

1 onion, finely chopped

1 bay leaf

⅔ cup dry white wine

⅔ cup sieved tomatoes

1 tbsp tomato paste

salt and pepper

fresh basil leaves, to garnish

1 Grease four ¾-cup molds or ramekins with the butter. Evenly coat the insides with half of the breadcrumbs.

2 Bring a pan of lightly salted water to a boil. Add the spaghetti and olive oil and cook for 8–10 minutes, or until just tender. Drain and transfer to a mixing bowl. Add the egg yolk and cheese to the pasta and season.

3 Pour the Béchamel Sauce into the bowl containing the pasta and mix. Spoon the mixture into the molds and sprinkle over the remaining breadcrumbs.

4 Stand the molds on a cookie sheet and bake in a preheated oven, 425°F/220°C, for 20 minutes. Set aside for 10 minutes.

5 Meanwhile, make the tomato sauce. Heat the oil in a pan and gently cook the onion and bay leaf for 2–3 minutes, stirring constantly.

6 Stir in the wine, sieved tomatoes, and tomato paste, and season to taste. Simmer for 20 minutes, until thickened. Remove and discard the bay leaf. Turn the timballini out on to serving plates, garnish with the basil leaves and serve with the tomato sauce.

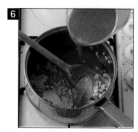

Pasta with Bacon & Tomatoes

As this dish cooks, the mouth-watering aroma of bacon, sweet tomatoes, and oregano is a feast in itself.

NUTRITIONAL INFORMATION

Calories	431	Sugars	8g
Protein	10g	Fat	9g
Carbohydrate	34g	Saturates	14g

🔪 10 mins   ⏱ 35 mins

SERVES 4

INGREDIENTS

2 lb/900 g small, sweet tomatoes

6 slices rindless smoked bacon

4 tbsp butter

1 onion, chopped

1 garlic clove, crushed

4 fresh oregano sprigs, finely chopped

1 lb/450 g dried orecchiette

1 tbsp olive oil

salt and pepper

freshly grated romano cheese, to serve

1 Blanch the tomatoes in boiling water. Drain, skin, and seed the tomatoes, then roughly chop the flesh.

2 Using a sharp knife, chop the bacon into evenly sized small dice.

3 Melt the butter in a pan. Add the bacon and cook until it is golden.

4 Add the onion and garlic and cook over a medium heat for 5–7 minutes, until just softened.

5 Add the tomatoes and oregano to the pan and then season to taste with salt and pepper. Lower the heat and simmer gently for 10–12 minutes.

6 Bring a large pan of lightly salted water to a boil. Add the orecchiette and oil and cook for 12 minutes, or until just tender, but firm to the bite. Drain the pasta and transfer to a warm serving bowl.

7 Spoon the bacon and tomato sauce over the pasta, toss to coat and serve with the romano cheese.

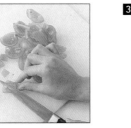

COOK'S TIP

For an authentic Italian flavor use pancetta, rather than ordinary bacon. Pancetta is streaked with fat and adds rich undertones of flavor to many traditional dishes. It is available smoked or unsmoked from large stores and delicatessens.

Spaghetti with Ricotta Cheese

This nutty pasta dish has a delicate flavor which is ideally suited to a light summer lunch.

NUTRITIONAL INFORMATION

Calories	714	Sugars	6g
Protein	22g	Fat	41g
Carbohydrate	69g	Saturates	14g

5 mins

5–10 mins

SERVES 4

INGREDIENTS

12 oz/ 350 g dried spaghetti

3 tbsp olive oil

3 tbsp butter

2 tbsp chopped fresh flatleaf parsley

1 cup freshly ground almonds

½ cup ricotta cheese

pinch of grated nutmeg

pinch of ground cinnamon

⅔ cup unsweetened yogurt

½ cup hot chicken bouillon

1 tbsp pine nuts

salt and pepper

fresh flatleaf parsley sprigs, to garnish

1 Bring a large pan of lightly salted water to a boil. Add the spaghetti and 1 tablespoon of the oil and cook until tender, but still firm to the bite.

2 Drain the pasta, return to the pan and toss with the butter and chopped parsley. Set aside and keep warm.

3 To make the sauce, mix together the ground almonds, ricotta cheese, nutmeg, cinnamon, and unsweetened yogurt over a low heat until it forms a thick paste. Gradually stir in the remaining oil. When the oil has been fully incorporated into the mixture, gradually stir in the hot chicken bouillon, until smooth. Season to taste with black pepper.

4 Transfer the spaghetti to a warm serving dish, pour over the sauce and toss together well (see Cook's Tip, right). Sprinkle over the pine nuts, garnish with the flatleaf parsley and serve warm.

COOK'S TIP

Use two large forks to toss spaghetti, so that it is thoroughly coated with the sauce. Ease the prongs under the pasta on each side and lift them towards the center. Continue this evenly and rhythmically until the pasta is completely coated.

Smoked Salmon Spaghetti

Made in moments, this is a luxurious dish which can be used to astonish and delight any unexpected guests.

NUTRITIONAL INFORMATION

Calories	 949	Sugars	.... 6g
Protein	.... 26g	Fat	.... 49g
Carbohydrate	.. 86g	Saturates	..... 27g

🏠 🏠 🏠

🥘 5–10 mins   🕐 5 mins

SERVES 4

INGREDIENTS

1 lb/450 g dried buckwheat spaghetti

2 tbsp olive oil

1¼ cups heavy cream

⅔ cup whiskey or brandy

4½ oz/125 g smoked salmon

pinch of cayenne pepper

black pepper

2 tbsp chopped fresh cilantro or parsley

½ cup feta cheese, well drained
    and crumbled

fresh cilantro or parsley leaves, to garnish

1 Bring a large pan of lightly salted water to a boil. Add the spaghetti and 1 tablespoon of the olive oil and cook until tender, but still firm to the bite. Drain the spaghetti, return to the pan and sprinkle over the remaining olive oil. Cover, shake the pan, set aside and keep warm.

2 Pour the cream into a small pan and bring to simmering point, but do not let it boil. Pour the whiskey or brandy into another small pan and bring to simmering point, but do not allow it to boil. Remove both pans from the heat and mix together the cream and whisky or brandy.

3 Cut the smoked salmon into thin strips and add to the cream mixture. Season to taste with cayenne and black pepper. Just before serving, stir in the chopped fresh cilantro.

4 Transfer the spaghetti to a warm serving dish, pour over the sauce and toss thoroughly with 2 large forks. Scatter over the crumbled feta cheese, garnish with the cilantro or parsley leaves and serve immediately.

COOK'S TIP

Serve this rich and luxurious dish with salad greens tossed in a lemon-flavored dressing.

Spaghetti Olio e Aglio

This easy and satisfying Roman dish originated as a cheap meal for poor people, but has now become a favorite in restaurants and trattorias.

NUTRITIONAL INFORMATION

Calories	515	Sugars	........1g
Protein	........8g	Fat	..........33g
Carbohydrate	..50g	Saturates	......5g

5 mins   5 mins

SERVES 4

INGREDIENTS

½ cup olive oil

3 garlic cloves, crushed

1 lb/450 g fresh spaghetti

3 tbsp roughly chopped fresh parsley

salt and pepper

1 Reserve 1 tablespoon of the olive oil and heat the remainder in a medium pan. Add the garlic and a pinch of salt and cook over a low heat, stirring constantly, until golden brown, then remove the pan from the heat. Do not allow the garlic to burn as it will taint the flavor. (If it does burn, you will have to start all over again!)

2 Meanwhile, bring a large pan of lightly salted water to a boil. Add the spaghetti and reserved olive oil to the pan and cook for 2–3 minutes, or until tender, but still firm to the bite. Drain the spaghetti thoroughly and return to the pan.

3 Add the oil and garlic mixture to the spaghetti and toss to coat thoroughly. Season with pepper, add the chopped fresh parsley and toss to coat again.

4 Transfer the spaghetti to a warm serving dish and serve immediately.

Braised Fennel & Linguine

The anise flavor of the fennel gives that little extra punch to this delicious, creamy, pasta dish.

NUTRITIONAL INFORMATION

Calories ...... 650 Sugars 6g
Protein .... 14g Fat 39g
Carbohydrate .. 62g Saturates 22g

20 mins

50 mins

SERVES 4

INGREDIENTS

6 fennel bulbs

⅔ cup vegetable bouillon

2 tbsp butter

6 slices rindless smoked bacon, diced

6 shallots, quartered

3 tbsp all-purpose flour

scant ½ cup heavy cream

1 tbsp Madeira

1 lb/450 g dried linguine

1 tbsp olive oil

salt and pepper

1 Trim the fennel bulbs, then peel off and reserve the outer layer of each. Cut the bulbs into quarters and put them in a large pan with the bouillon and the reserved outer layers.

2 Bring to a boil, lower the heat and simmer for 5 minutes.

3 Using a perforated spoon, transfer the fennel to a large dish. Discard the outer layers of the fennel bulbs. Bring the vegetable bouillon to a boil and allow to reduce by half. Set aside.

4 Melt the butter in a skillet. Add the bacon and shallots and cook over a medium heat, stirring frequently, for 4 minutes. Add the flour, reduced bouillon, cream, and Madeira and cook, stirring constantly, for 3 minutes, or until the sauce is smooth. Season to taste with salt and pepper and pour over the fennel.

5 Bring a large pan of lightly salted water to a boil. Add the linguine and olive oil, bring back to a boil and cook for 8–10 minutes, or until tender, but still firm to the bite. Drain and transfer to a deep ovenproof dish.

6 Add the fennel and sauce and cook in a preheated oven, 350°F/180°C, for 20 minutes. Serve immediately.

COOK'S TIP

Fennel will keep in the salad drawer of the refrigerator for 2–3 days, but it is best eaten as fresh as possible. Cut surfaces turn brown quickly, so do not prepare it too much in advance of cooking.

Pasta Omelet

This is a superb way of using up any leftover pasta, such as penne, macaroni, or conchiglie.

NUTRITIONAL INFORMATION

Calories 638   Sugars 5g
Protein .... 24g   Fat 38g
Carbohydrate .. 53g   Saturates 7g

🕒 5 mins   ⏰ 15–20 mins

SERVES 2

INGREDIENTS

4 tbsp olive oil

1 small onion, chopped

1 fennel bulb, thinly sliced

generous ⅔ cup diced potato

1 garlic clove, chopped

4 eggs

1 tbsp chopped fresh flatleaf parsley

pinch of chili powder

3½ oz/100 g cooked short pasta

2 tbsp stuffed green olives, halved

salt and pepper

fresh marjoram sprigs, to garnish

tomato salad, to serve

4 Heat 1 tablespoon of the remaining oil in a clean skillet. Add half of the egg mixture to the pan, then add the cooked vegetables, pasta, and half of the olives. Pour in the remaining egg mixture and cook until the sides begin to set.

5 Lift up the edges of the omelet with a spatula to allow the uncooked egg to spread underneath. Cook, shaking the pan occasionally, until the underside is a light golden brown color.

6 Slide the omelet out of the pan on to a plate. Wipe the pan with paper towels and heat the remaining oil. Invert the omelet into the pan and cook until the other side is golden brown.

7 Slide the omelet on to a warmed serving dish and garnish with the remaining olives and the marjoram. Serve cut into wedges, with a tomato salad.

1 Heat half the oil in a heavy-based skillet over a low heat. Add the onion, fennel, and potato and cook, stirring occasionally, for 8–10 minutes, until the potato is just tender.

2 Stir in the chopped garlic and cook for 1 minute. Remove the pan from the heat, transfer the vegetables to a plate, and set aside to keep warm.

3 Beat the eggs until they are frothy. Stir in the parsley and season with salt, pepper and a pinch of chili powder.

Fettuccine all'Alfredo

This simple, traditional dish can be made with any long pasta, but is especially good with flat noodles, such as fettuccine or tagliatelle.

NUTRITIONAL INFORMATION

Calories	540	Sugars	2g
Protein	15g	Fat	40g
Carbohydrate	31g	Saturates	23g

5 mins   5 mins

SERVES 4

INGREDIENTS

2 tbsp butter

scant 1 cup heavy cream

1 lb/450 g fresh fettuccine

1 tbsp olive oil

1 cup freshly grated Parmesan cheese, plus extra to serve

pinch of freshly grated nutmeg

fresh flatleaf parsley sprig, to garnish

salt and pepper

2 Meanwhile, bring a large pan of lightly salted water to a boil. Add the fettuccine and olive oil and cook for 2–3 minutes, or until tender, but still firm to the bite. Drain the fettuccine thoroughly and return it to the warm pan, then pour over the cream sauce.

3 Toss the fettuccine in the sauce over a low heat until thoroughly coated.

4 Add the remaining cream and the Parmesan cheese and nutmeg to the fettuccine mixture, and season to taste with salt and pepper. Toss thoroughly to coat while gently heating through.

5 Transfer the fettucine mixture to a warm serving plate and garnish with fresh parsley. Serve immediately, handing extra grated Parmesan cheese separately.

1 Put the butter and ²⁄₃ cup of the cream in a large pan and bring the mixture to a boil over a medium heat. Reduce the heat and simmer gently for about 1½ minutes, or until slightly thickened.

VARIATION

This classic Roman dish is often served with the addition of strips of ham and fresh peas. Add 2 cups shelled cooked peas and 6 oz/175 g ham strips with the Parmesan cheese in step 4.

Pistou

This hearty soup of beans and vegetables is from Nice and gets its name from the fresh basil sauce stirred in at the last minute.

NUTRITIONAL INFORMATION

Calories	55	Sugars	1.2g
Protein	3.8g	Fat	2.6g
Carbohydrate	4.2g	Saturates	0.6g

🥔 10 mins 🕐 25 mins

SERVES 6

I N G R E D I E N T S

2 young carrots

1 lb/450 g potatoes

7 oz/200 g fresh peas in their shells

7 oz/200 g thin green beans

5½ oz/150 g young zucchini

2 tbsp olive oil

1 garlic clove, crushed

1 large onion, finely chopped

12 cups vegetable bouillon or water

1 bouquet garni or 2 fresh parsley sprigs and 1 bay leaf tied in a 3 inch/7.5 cm piece of celery stalk

3 oz/85 g dried small soup pasta

1 large tomato, skinned, deseeded, and chopped or diced

pared Parmesan cheese, to serve

PISTOU SAUCE

2¾ oz/75 g fresh basil leaves

1 garlic clove

5 tbsp fruity extra-virgin olive oil

salt and pepper

1 To make the pistou sauce, put the basil leaves, garlic, and olive oil in a food processor and process until well blended. Season with salt and pepper to taste. Transfer to a bowl, cover with plastic wrap and chill until required.

2 Peel the carrots, cut them in half lengthwise, then slice them. Peel the potatoes and cut into quarters lengthwise, then slice. Set aside in a bowl of water until ready to use, to prevent discoloration.

3 Shell the fresh peas. Trim the green beans and cut them into 1 inch/ 2.5 cm pieces. Cut the zucchini in half lengthwise, then slice crosswise.

4 Heat the oil in a large pan or flameproof casserole. Add the garlic and cook for 2 minutes, stirring. Add the onion and continue cooking for 2 minutes until soft. Add the carrots and potatoes and stir for about 30 seconds.

5 Pour in the bouillon and bring to a boil. Lower the heat, partially cover, and simmer for 8 minutes, until the vegetables are starting to become tender.

6 Stir in the peas, beans, zucchini, bouquet garni, pasta, and tomato. Season and cook for 4 minutes, or until the vegetables and pasta are tender. Stir in the pistou sauce and serve with Parmesan.

Spinach & Herb Orzo

Serve this vibrant green pasta dish with any broiled meat or seafood.
Orzo, shaped like grains of barley, is popular in southern Italy and Greece.

NUTRITIONAL INFORMATION

Calories	304	Sugars	8g
Protein	12g	Fat	6g
Carbohydrate	54g	Saturates	1g

15–20 mins 10 mins

SERVES 4

INGREDIENTS

1 tsp salt

9 oz/250 g dried orzo

7 oz/200 g baby spinach leaves

5½ oz/150 g arugula

1 oz/25 g fresh flatleaf parsley leaves

1 oz/25 g fresh cilantro leaves

4 scallions

2 tbsp extra-virgin olive oil

1 tbsp garlic-flavored olive oil

pepper

TO SERVE

radicchio or other lettuce leaves

2 oz/60 g feta cheese, well drained and crumbled (optional)

lemon slices

3 Put the spinach, arugula, parsley, cilantro, and scallions in the other pan of boiling water and blanch for 15 seconds. Drain and transfer to the iced water to preserve the color.

4 When the spinach, herbs, and scallions are cool, squeeze out all the excess water. Transfer to a small food processor and process. Add the olive oil and garlic-flavored oil and process again until the spinach mixture is well blended.

5 Drain the orzo well and stir in the spinach mixture. Toss well and adjust the seasoning.

6 Line a serving platter with radicchio leaves and pile the orzo on top. Sprinkle with feta cheese, if desired, and garnish with lemon slices. Serve hot or let cool to room temperature.

1 Bring 2 pans of water to a boil, and put 12 ice cubes in a bowl of cold water. Add the salt and orzo to one of the pans, return to a boil and cook for 8–10 minutes, or according to packet instructions, until the pasta is tender.

2 Meanwhile, remove any tough spinach stems. Rinse the leaves thoroughly to remove any grit. Chop the arugula, parsley, cilantro, and green parts of the scallions.

Brown Lentil & Pasta Soup

In Italy, this soup is called *Minestrade Lentiche*. A minestra is a soup cooked with pasta; here, farfalline, a small bow-shaped variety, is used.

NUTRITIONAL INFORMATION

Calories 225	Sugars 1g
Protein 13g	Fat 8g
Carbohydrate . . 27g	Saturates 3g

5 mins   25 mins

SERVES 4

I N G R E D I E N T S

4 slices lean bacon, cut into small squares

1 onion, chopped

2 garlic cloves, crushed

2 celery stalks, chopped

1¾ oz/50 g farfalline or spaghetti, broken into small pieces

14 oz/400 g canned brown lentils, drained

5 cups hot ham or vegetable bouillon

2 tbsp chopped fresh mint

1 Place the bacon in a large skillet together with the onions, garlic, and celery. Dry cook for 4–5 minutes, stirring, until the onion is tender and the bacon is just beginning to brown.

2 Add the pasta to the skillet and cook, stirring, for about 1 minute, to coat the pasta thoroughly in the oil.

3 Add the brown lentils and the ham or vegetable bouillon and bring the mixture to a boil. Reduce the heat and leave to simmer for 12–15 minutes, or until the pasta is tender.

4 Remove the skillet from the heat and stir in the chopped fresh mint.

5 Transfer the soup to warm soup bowls and serve immediately.

COOK'S TIP

If you prefer to use dried lentils, add the bouillon before the pasta and cook for 1–1¼ hours until the lentils are tender. Add the pasta and cook for a further 12–15 minutes.

Italian Fish Stew

This robust stew is full of Mediterranean flavors. If you do not want to prepare the fish yourself, ask your local fishmonger to do it for you.

NUTRITIONAL INFORMATION

Calories 236   Sugars 4g
Protein .... 20g   Fat 7g
Carbohydrate .. 25g   Saturates 1g

5–10 mins   25 mins

SERVES 4

INGREDIENTS

2 tbsp olive oil

2 red onions, finely chopped

1 garlic clove, crushed

2 zucchini, sliced

14 oz/400 g canned chopped tomatoes

3½ cups fish or vegetable bouillon

3 oz/90 g dried pasta shapes

12 oz/350 g firm white fish, such as cod, haddock, or hake

1 tbsp chopped fresh basil or oregano or 1 tsp dried oregano

1 tsp grated lemon zest

1 tbsp cornstarch

1 tbsp water

salt and pepper

sprigs of fresh basil or oregano, to garnish

3 Skin and bone the fish, then cut it into chunks. Add the fish chunks to the pan with the basil or oregano and lemon zest and cook gently for 5 minutes, until the fish is opaque and flakes easily (take care not to overcook it).

4 Blend the cornstarch with the water and stir into the stew. Cook gently for 2 minutes, stirring, until thickened. Season with salt and pepper to taste and ladle into warmed soup bowls. Garnish with basil or oregano sprigs and serve at once.

1 Heat the oil in a large pan and cook the onions and garlic for 5 minutes. Add the zucchini and continue to cook for 2–3 minutes, stirring often.

2 Add the tomatoes and bouillon to the pan and bring to a boil. Add the pasta, cover the pan, and reduce the heat. Simmer for 5 minutes.

Spinach & Anchovy Pasta

This colorful, light meal can be made with a variety of different pasta, including spaghetti and linguine.

NUTRITIONAL INFORMATION

Calories	 619	Sugars	.... 5g
Protein	.... 21g	Fat	.... 31g
Carbohydrate	.. 67g	Saturates	...... 3g

10 mins   25 mins

SERVES 4

I N G R E D I E N T S

2 lb/900 g fresh, young spinach leaves

14 oz/400 g dried fettuccine

6 tbsp olive oil

3 tbsp pine nuts

3 garlic cloves, crushed

8 canned anchovy fillets, drained and chopped

salt

1 Trim off any tough spinach stalks. Rinse the spinach leaves and place them in a large pan with only the water that is clinging to them after washing. Cover and cook over a high heat, shaking the pan from time, until the spinach has wilted, but retains its bright green color. Drain well, set aside and keep warm.

2 Bring a large pan of lightly salted water to a boil. Add the fettuccine and 1 tablespoon of the olive oil and cook for 8–10 minutes, or until just tender, but still firm to the bite.

3 Heat 4 tablespoons of the remaining olive oil in a pan. Add the pine nuts and cook until golden brown. Remove the pine nuts from the pan and set aside.

4 Add the garlic to the pan and cook until golden. Add the anchovies and stir in the spinach. Cook, stirring, for 2–3 minutes, until heated through. Return the pine nuts to the pan.

5 Drain the fettuccine, toss in the remaining olive oil, and transfer to a warm serving dish. Spoon the anchovy and spinach sauce over the fettucine, toss lightly, and serve immediately.

COOK'S TIP

If you are in a hurry, you can use frozen leaf spinach. Thaw and drain it thoroughly, pressing out as much moisture as possible. Cut the leaves into strips and add to the dish with the anchovies in step 4.

Spaghetti Bolognese

You can use this classic meat sauce for lasagna, cannelloni, or any other baked pasta dishes.

NUTRITIONAL INFORMATION

Calories	732	Sugars	15g
Protein	39g	Fat	20g
Carbohydrate	96g	Saturates	5g

5 mins   1¼ hrs

SERVES 4

3 tbsp olive oil

2 garlic cloves, crushed

1 large onion, finely chopped

1 carrot, diced

2 cups lean ground beef, veal, or chicken

3 oz/85 g chicken livers, finely chopped

3½ oz/100 g lean prosciutto, diced

⅔ cup Marsala

10 oz/280 g canned chopped
    plum tomatoes

1 tbsp chopped fresh basil leaves

2 tbsp tomato paste

salt and pepper

1 lb/450 g dried spaghetti

1 Heat 2 tablespoons of the olive oil in a large pan. Add the garlic, onion, and carrot, and cook for 6 minutes.

2 Add the ground beef, veal, or chicken, chicken livers, and prosciutto, to the pan, and cook over a medium heat for 12 minutes, until well browned.

3 Stir in the Marsala, tomatoes, basil, and tomato paste and cook, stirring, for 4 minutes. Season to taste with salt and pepper. Cover the pan and simmer for about 30 minutes.

4 Remove the lid from the pan, stir, and simmer for a further 15 minutes.

5 Meanwhile, bring a large pan of lightly salted water to a boil. Add the spaghetti and the remaining oil and cook for about 12 minutes, or until tender, but still firm to the bite. Drain and transfer to a serving dish. Pour the sauce over the pasta, toss, and serve hot.

VARIATION

Chicken livers are an essential ingredient in a classic Bolognese sauce, to which they add richness. However, if you prefer not to use them, you can substitute the same quantity of ground beef.

Creamed Strips of Short Loin

This quick and easy dish tastes superb and would make a delicious treat for a special occasion.

NUTRITIONAL INFORMATION

Calories 796   Sugars 2g
Protein .... 29g   Fat 63g
Carbohydrate .. 26g   Saturates 39g

15 mins   30 mins

SERVES 4

INGREDIENTS

6 tbsp butter

1 lb/450 g short loin steak, trimmed, and cut into thin strips

6 oz/175 g white mushrooms, sliced

1 tsp mustard

pinch of freshly grated ginger root

2 tbsp dry sherry

⅔ cup heavy cream

salt and pepper

4 slices hot toast, cut into triangles, to serve

PASTA

1 lb/450 g dried rigatoni

2 tbsp olive oil

2 fresh basil sprigs

½ cup butter

1 Melt the butter in a large skillet and gently cook the steak over a low heat, stirring frequently, for 6 minutes. Using a slotted spoon, transfer the steak to an ovenproof dish and keep warm.

2 Add the sliced mushrooms to the skillet and cook for 2–3 minutes in the juices remaining in the pan. Add the mustard, ginger, salt, and pepper. Cook for 2 minutes, then add the sherry and cream. Cook for a further 3 minutes, then pour the cream sauce over the steak.

3 Bake the steak and cream sauce mixture in a preheated oven, 375°F/190°C, for 10 minutes.

4 Meanwhile, bring a large pan of lightly salted water to a boil. Add the rigatoni, olive oil, and 1 of the basil sprigs, and boil rapidly for 10 minutes, or until tender, but firm to the bite. Drain the pasta and transfer to a warm serving plate. Toss the pasta with the butter and garnish with the other sprig of basil.

5 Serve the creamed steak strips with the pasta and triangles of hot toast.

COOK'S TIP

Dried pasta will keep for up to 6 months. Keep it in the packet and reseal it once you have opened it, or transfer it to an airtight jar.

Fresh Spaghetti & Meatballs

This well-loved Italian dish is famous across the world. Make the most of it by using high-quality steak for the meatballs.

NUTRITIONAL INFORMATION

Calories 665   Sugars 9g
Protein .... 39g   Fat 24g
Carbohydrate .. 77g   Saturates 8g

45 mins   1¼ hrs

SERVES 4

INGREDIENTS

2½ cups brown bread crumbs

⅔ cup milk

2 tbsp butter

3 tbsp whole-wheat flour

scant 1 cup beef bouillon

14 oz/400 g canned chopped tomatoes

2 tbsp tomato paste

1 tsp sugar

1 tbsp finely chopped fresh tarragon

1 large onion, chopped

4 cups ground steak

1 tsp paprika

4 tbsp olive oil

1 lb/450 g fresh spaghetti

salt and pepper

fresh tarragon sprigs, to garnish

1 Place the brown bread crumbs in a bowl, add the milk and set aside to soak for about 30 minutes.

2 Melt half of the butter in a pan. Add the flour and cook, stirring constantly, for 2 minutes. Gradually stir in the beef bouillon and cook, stirring constantly, for a further 5 minutes. Add the tomatoes, tomato paste, sugar, and tarragon. Season well and simmer for 25 minutes.

3 Mix the onion, steak, and paprika into the breadcrumbs, and season with salt and pepper to taste. Shape the mixture into 14 meatballs.

4 Heat the oil and remaining butter in a skillet and cook the meatballs, turning, until brown all over. Place in a deep casserole, pour over the tomato sauce, cover and bake in a preheated oven, 350°F/180°C, for 25 minutes.

5 Bring a large pan of lightly salted water to a boil. Add the fresh spaghetti, bring back to a boil, and cook for about 2–3 minutes, or until tender, but firm to the bite.

6 Meanwhile, remove the meatballs from the oven and let cool for 3 minutes. Serve the meatballs and their sauce with the spaghetti, garnished with fresh tarragon sprigs.

Pasticcio

A recipe that has both Italian and Greek origins, this dish may be served hot or cold, cut into thick, satisfying squares.

NUTRITIONAL INFORMATION

Calories	590	Sugars	8g
Protein	34g	Fat	39g
Carbohydrate	23g	Saturates	16g

35 mins   1¼ hrs

SERVES 6

I N G R E D I E N T S

8 oz/225 g fusilli, or other short pasta shapes

1 tbsp olive oil

4 tbsp heavy cream

rosemary sprigs, to garnish

SAUCE

2 tbsp olive oil, plus extra for brushing

1 onion, thinly sliced

1 red bell pepper, deseeded and chopped

2 garlic cloves, chopped

1 lb 6 oz/625 g lean ground beef

14 oz/400 g canned chopped tomatoes

½ cup dry white wine

2 tbsp chopped fresh parsley

1¾ oz/50 g canned anchovies, drained and chopped

salt and pepper

TOPPING

1¼ cups plain yogurt

3 eggs

pinch of freshly grated nutmeg

½ cup freshly grated Parmesan cheese

1 To make the sauce, heat the oil in a large skillet and cook the onion and red bell pepper for 3 minutes. Stir in the garlic and cook for 1 minute more. Stir in the beef and cook, stirring frequently, until it is no longer pink.

2 Add the tomatoes and wine to the pan, stir well and bring to a boil. Simmer, uncovered, for 20 minutes, or until the sauce is fairly thick. Stir in the parsley and anchovies and season to taste.

3 Cook the pasta in plenty of boiling salted water, adding the oil, for 8–10 minutes, or until tender. Drain and transfer to a bowl. Stir in the cream and set aside.

4 To make the topping, beat together the yogurt, eggs, and nutmeg until they are well combined, and season with salt and pepper to taste.

5 Brush a large, shallow ovenproof dish with oil. Spoon in half of the pasta mixture and cover with half of the meat sauce. Repeat these layers, then spread the topping evenly over the final layer. Sprinkle the grated Parmesan cheese evenly on top.

6 Bake in a preheated oven, 375°F/ 190°C, for 25 minutes, or until the topping is golden brown and bubbling. Garnish with sprigs of fresh rosemary and serve immediately.

Neapolitan Veal Cutlets

The delicious combination of apple, onion, and mushroom perfectly complements the delicate flavor of veal.

NUTRITIONAL INFORMATION

Calories	1071	Sugars	13g
Protein	74g	Fat	59g
Carbohydrate	66g	Saturates	16g

20 mins   45 mins

SERVES 4

INGREDIENTS

scant 1 cup butter

4 x 9 oz/250 g veal cutlets, trimmed

1 large onion, sliced

2 apples, peeled, cored, and sliced

6 oz/175 g white mushrooms

1 tbsp chopped fresh tarragon

8 black peppercorns

1 tbsp sesame seeds

14 oz/400 g dried marille

scant ½ cup extra virgin olive oil

2 large beefsteak tomatoes, cut in half

¾ cup mascarpone cheese

leaves of 1 fresh basil sprig

salt and pepper

fresh basil leaves, to garnish

3 Melt the remaining butter in the skillet. Gently cook the mushrooms, tarragon, and peppercorns over a low heat for 3 minutes. Sprinkle the sesame seeds over the gently cooking ingredients.

4 Bring a pan of salted water to the boil. Add the pasta and 1 tablespoon of oil. Cook for 8–10 minutes, or until tender, but firm to the bite. Drain. Transfer to a plate.

5 Grill or fry the halved tomatoes with the basil for 2–3 minutes.

6 Top the pasta with the mascarpone cheese and sprinkle over the remaining olive oil. Place the onions, apples, and veal cutlets on top of the pasta. Spoon the mushrooms, peppercorns, and the pan juices on to the cutlets, arrange the tomatoes and basil leaves around the edge, and place in a preheated oven, 300°F/150°C, for 5 minutes.

7 Season to taste with salt and pepper, garnish with fresh basil leaves and serve immediately.

1 Melt 4 tablespoons of the butter in a skillet. Cook the veal over a low heat for 5 minutes on each side. Transfer to a dish and keep warm.

2 Cook the onion and apples in the pan until lightly browned. Transfer to a dish, place the veal on top and keep warm.

Tagliatelle with Pumpkin

This unusual dish comes from the Emilia Romagna region. Why not serve it with Lambrusco, the local wine?

NUTRITIONAL INFORMATION

Calories	559	Sugars	7g
Protein	17g	Fat	32g
Carbohydrate	55g	Saturates	14g

5 mins

20–25 mins

SERVES 4

INGREDIENTS

1 lb 2 oz/500 g pumpkin or butternut squash, peeled and deseeded

3 tbsp olive oil

1 onion, finely chopped

2 garlic cloves, crushed

4–6 tbsp chopped fresh parsley

pinch of freshly grated nutmeg

about 1¼ cups chicken or vegetable bouillon

4 oz/115 g prosciutto, cut into small pieces

9 oz/250 g dried tagliatelle

⅔ cup heavy cream

salt and pepper

freshly grated Parmesan cheese, to serve

3 Add the pumpkin or squash pieces and cook for 2–3 minutes. Season to taste with salt, pepper, and nutmeg.

4 Add half the bouillon to the pan, bring to a boil, cover, and simmer for about 10 minutes, or until the pumpkin or squash is tender. Add more bouillon if the pumpkin or squash is becoming dry and looks as if it might be about to burn.

5 Add the prosciutto to the pan and cook, stirring, for a further 2 minutes.

6 Meanwhile, bring a large pan of lightly salted water to a boil. Add the tagliatelle and the remaining oil and cook for 12 minutes, or until tender, but still firm to the bite. Drain the pasta and transfer to a warm serving dish.

7 Stir the cream into the pumpkin and ham mixture and heat well through. Spoon the mixture over the tagliatelle, sprinkle over the remaining parsley to garnish and serve while still hot. Hand the grated Parmesan separately.

1 Cut the pumpkin or butternut squash in half and scoop out the seeds with a spoon. Cut the pumpkin or squash into ½ inch/1 cm dice.

2 Heat 2 tablespoons of the olive oil in a large pan. Add the onion and garlic and cook over a low heat for about 3 minutes, until soft. Add half the parsley and cook for 1 minute.

Chicken Suprême Spaghetti

The refreshing combination of chicken and orange sauce makes this a perfect dish for a warm summer evening.

NUTRITIONAL INFORMATION

Calories	 933	Sugars	.... 34g
Protein	.... 74g	Fat	.... 24g
Carbohydrate	. 100g	Saturates	...... 5g

5 mins   20 mins

SERVES 4

INGREDIENTS

2 tbsp rapeseed oil

3 tbsp olive oil

4 x 8 oz/225 g chicken suprêmes

²⁄₃ cup orange brandy

2 tbsp all-purpose flour

²⁄₃ cup freshly squeezed orange juice

1 oz/25 g zucchini, cut into very thin strips

1 oz/25 g leek, finely shredded

1 oz/25 g red bell pepper, cut into very thin strips

14 oz/400 g dried whole-wheat spaghetti

3 large oranges, peeled and cut into segments

rind of 1 orange, cut into very thin strips

2 tbsp chopped fresh tarragon

²⁄₃ cup ricotta cheese

salt and pepper

fresh tarragon leaves, to garnish

1 Heat the rapeseed oil and 1 tablespoon of the olive oil in a skillet. Add the chicken and cook quickly until golden brown. Add the orange brandy and cook for 3 minutes. Sprinkle over the flour and cook for 2 minutes.

2 Lower the heat and add the orange juice, zucchini, leek, and bell pepper, and season. Simmer for 5 minutes until the sauce has thickened.

3 Meanwhile, bring a pan of salted water to a boil. Add the spaghetti and 1 tablespoon of the olive oil and cook for 10 minutes. Drain, transfer to a serving dish, and drizzle over the remaining oil.

4 Add half the orange segments, half the orange rind strips, the tarragon, and the ricotta cheese to the sauce in the pan, and cook for 3 minutes.

5 Place the chicken on top of the pasta, pour over a little sauce, garnish with the remaining orange segments and rind, and tarragon and serve immediately.

Pasta with Chicken Sauce

Spinach ribbon noodles, topped with a rich tomato sauce and creamy chicken, make a very appetizing dish.

NUTRITIONAL INFORMATION

Calories 995	Sugars 8g	
Protein 36g	Fat 74g	
Carbohydrate .. 50g	Saturates 34g	

15 mins   45 mins

SERVES 4

INGREDIENTS

9 oz/250 g fresh green tagliatelle

1 tbsp olive oil

fresh basil leaves, to garnish

TOMATO SAUCE

2 tbsp olive oil

1 small onion, chopped

1 garlic clove, chopped

14 oz/400 g canned chopped tomatoes

2 tbsp chopped fresh parsley

1 tsp dried oregano

2 bay leaves

2 tbsp tomato paste

1 tsp sugar

salt and pepper

CHICKEN SAUCE

4 tbsp unsalted butter

14 oz/400 g boned chicken breasts, skinned and cut into thin strips

¾ cup blanched almonds

1¼ cups heavy cream

salt and pepper

1 To make the tomato sauce, heat the oil in a pan over a medium heat. Add the onion and cook until translucent. Add the garlic and cook for 1 minute. Stir in the tomatoes, parsley, oregano, bay leaves, tomato paste, sugar, and salt and pepper to taste, bring to a boil and simmer, uncovered, for 15–20 minutes, until reduced by half. Remove the pan from the heat and discard the bay leaves.

2 To make the chicken sauce, gently melt the butter in a skillet over a medium heat. Add the chicken and almonds and stir-fry for 5–6 minutes, or until the chicken is cooked through.

3 Meanwhile, bring the cream to a boil in a small pan over a low heat and boil for about 10 minutes, until reduced by almost half. Pour the cream over the chicken and almonds, stir, and season to taste with salt and pepper. Set aside and keep warm.

4 Bring a large pan of lightly salted water to a boil. Add the tagliatelle and olive oil and cook for 8–10 minutes, or until tender, but still firm to the bite. Drain and transfer to a warm serving dish. Spoon over the tomato sauce and arrange the chicken sauce down the center. Garnish with the basil leaves and serve immediately.

Mustard Baked Chicken

Chicken pieces are cooked in a succulent, mild mustard sauce, then coated in poppy seeds and served on a bed of fresh pasta shells.

NUTRITIONAL INFORMATION

Calories	652	Sugars	5g
Protein	51g	Fat	31g
Carbohydrate	46g	Saturates	12g

10 mins   35 mins

SERVES 4

INGREDIENTS

8 x 4 oz/115 g chicken pieces

4 tbsp butter, melted

4 tbsp mild mustard (see Cook's Tip)

2 tbsp lemon juice

1 tbsp brown sugar

1 tsp paprika

3 tbsp poppy seeds

14 oz/400 g fresh pasta shells

1 tbsp olive oil

salt and pepper

1 Arrange the chicken pieces in a single layer in a large ovenproof dish.

2 Mix together the butter, mustard, lemon juice, brown sugar, and paprika in a bowl, and season with salt and pepper to taste. Brush half of the mixture over the upper surfaces of the chicken pieces and bake in a preheated oven, 400°F/200°C, for 15 minutes.

3 Remove the dish from the oven and carefully turn over the chicken pieces. Coat the upper surfaces of the chicken with the remaining mustard mixture, sprinkle the chicken pieces with poppy seeds and return to the oven for a further 15 minutes.

4 Meanwhile, bring a large pan of lightly salted water to a boil. Add the pasta and olive oil and cook with the lid off for 8–10 minutes, or until the pasta is tender, but still firm to the bite.

5 Drain the pasta thoroughly and arrange on a warmed serving dish. Top the pasta with the chicken, pour over the sauce and serve immediately.

COOK'S TIP

Dijon is the type of mustard most often used in cooking, as it has a clean and only mildly spicy flavor. German mustard has a sweet-sour taste, and Bavarian mustard is slightly sweeter. American mustard is mild and sweet.

Chicken & Lobster on Penne

While this is certainly a treat to get the taste buds tingling, it is not as extravagant as it sounds.

NUTRITIONAL INFORMATION

Calories	696	Sugars	4g
Protein	59g	Fat	32g
Carbohydrate	45g	Saturates	9g

🍲 20 mins   🕐 30 mins

SERVES 6

I N G R E D I E N T S

butter, for greasing

6 chicken suprêmes

1 lb/450 g dried penne rigate

6 tbsp extra virgin olive oil

1 cup freshly grated Parmesan cheese

F I L L I N G

4 oz/115 g lobster meat, chopped

2 shallots, very finely chopped

2 figs, chopped

1 tbsp Marsala

2 tbsp breadcrumbs

1 large egg, beaten

salt and pepper

1 Grease 6 pieces of foil large enough to enclose each chicken suprême and lightly grease a cookie sheet.

2 Place all of the filling ingredients into a mixing bowl and blend together thoroughly with a spoon.

3 Cut a pocket in each chicken suprême with a sharp knife and fill with the lobster mixture. Wrap each chicken suprême in foil, place the foil parcels on the greased cookie sheet and bake in a preheated oven, 400°F/200°C, for 30 minutes.

4 Meanwhile, bring a large pan of lightly salted water to a boil. Add the pasta and 1 tablespoon of the olive oil and cook for about 10 minutes, or until tender, but still firm to the bite. Drain the pasta thoroughly and transfer to a large serving plate. Sprinkle over the remaining olive oil and the grated Parmesan cheese, set aside and keep warm.

5 Carefully remove the foil from around the chicken suprêmes. Slice the suprêmes very thinly, arrange over the pasta and serve immediately.

COOK'S TIP

The cut of chicken known as suprême consists of the breast and wing. It is always skinned.

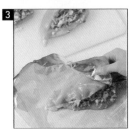

Slices of Duckling with Pasta

A raspberry and honey sauce superbly counterbalances the richness of tender slices of duckling.

NUTRITIONAL INFORMATION

Calories	686	Sugars	15g
Protein	62g	Fat	20g
Carbohydrate	70g	Saturates	7g

🐟 🐟 🐟

◆ 15 mins   ⏱ 25 mins

SERVES 4

INGREDIENTS

4 x 9 oz/275 g boned breasts of duckling

2 tbsp butter

scant ½ cup finely chopped carrots

4 tbsp finely chopped shallots

1 tbsp lemon juice

⅔ cup meat bouillon

4 tbsp clear honey

¾ cup fresh or thawed frozen raspberries

3 tbsp all-purpose flour

1 tbsp Worcestershire sauce

14 oz/400 g fresh linguine

1 tbsp olive oil

salt and pepper

TO GARNISH

fresh sprig of flatleaf parsley

fresh raspberries

1 Trim and score the duck breasts with a sharp knife and season well all over. Melt the butter in a skillet, add the duck breasts and cook them until they are lightly colored on both sides.

2 Add the carrots, shallots, lemon juice, and half the meat bouillon and simmer over a low heat for 1 minute. Stir in half of the honey and half of the raspberries. Sprinkle over half of the flour and cook, stirring constantly, for 3 minutes. Season with pepper to taste and add the Worcestershire sauce.

3 Stir in the remaining bouillon and cook for 1 minute. Stir in the remaining honey and the rest of the raspberries and sprinkle over the remaining flour. Cook for a further 3 minutes.

4 Remove the duck breasts and leave the sauce to simmer over a very low heat.

5 Meanwhile, bring a large pan of lightly salted water to a boil. Add the linguine and oil and cook for 8–10 minutes, or until tender, but firm to the bite. Drain and divide between individual plates.

6 Slice the duck breast lengthwise into ¼ inch/5 mm thick pieces. Pour a little sauce over the pasta and arrange the slices in a fan shape on top. Garnish with parsley and raspberries and serve immediately.

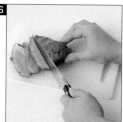

Pasta-Stuffed Tomatoes

This unusual and inexpensive dish would make a good appetizer for eight people or a delicious lunch for four.

NUTRITIONAL INFORMATION

Calories 298	Sugars 4g	
Protein 10g	Fat 20g	
Carbohydrate ...20g	Saturates 5g	

🍲 15 mins 🕐 35 mins

SERVES 4

INGREDIENTS

5 tbsp extra virgin olive oil, plus extra for greasing

8 beefsteak tomatoes or large round tomatoes

4 oz/115 g dried ditalini or other very small pasta shapes

8 black olives, pitted and finely chopped

2 tbsp finely chopped fresh basil

1 tbsp finely chopped fresh parsley

⅔ cup freshly grated Parmesan cheese

salt and pepper

fresh basil sprigs, to garnish

1 Prepare a cookie sheet by brushing with olive oil. Set aside.

2 Slice the tops off the tomatoes and reserve to make "lids". If the tomatoes will not stand up, cut a thin slice off the bottom of each tomato.

3 Using a teaspoon, scoop out the tomato pulp into a strainer, but do not pierce the tomato shells. Invert the tomato shells on to paper towels, pat dry, and set aside to drain.

4 Bring a large pan of lightly salted water to a boil. Add the ditalini or other pasta and 1 tablespoon of the remaining olive oil and cook for 8-10 minutes or until tender, but still firm to the bite. Drain the pasta and set aside.

5 Put the olives, basil, parsley, and Parmesan cheese into a large mixing bowl and stir in the strained tomato pulp. Add the pasta to the bowl. Stir in the remaining olive oil, mix together well, and season to taste with salt and pepper.

6 Arrange the tomatoes on the cookie sheet. Spoon the pasta mixture into the tomato shells and replace the lids. Bake in an oven preheated to 375°F/190°C, for 15-20 minutes.

7 Remove the tomatoes from the oven and let cool until just warm.

8 Arrange the pasta-stuffed tomatoes on a serving dish, garnish with the basil sprigs, and serve.

Venison Meatballs

The sharp, citrus-like flavor of kumquats is the perfect complement to these tasty steamed meatballs. Serve with pasta and fresh vegetables.

NUTRITIONAL INFORMATION

Calories 181	Sugars 8g	
Protein 26g	Fat 2g	
Carbohydrate ...11g	Saturates 1g	

🕑 5–10 mins   🕐 10 mins

SERVES 4

INGREDIENTS

1 lb/450 g lean ground venison

1 small leek, finely chopped

1 medium carrot, finely grated

½ tsp ground nutmeg

1 medium egg white, lightly beaten

salt and pepper

SAUCE

3½ oz/100 g kumquats

1 tbsp superfine sugar

⅔ cup water

4 tbsp dry sherry

1 tsp cornstarch

TO SERVE

freshly cooked pasta or noodles

freshly cooked vegetables

1 Place the venison in a mixing bowl together with the leek, carrot, seasoning, and nutmeg. Add the egg white and bind the ingredients together with your hands until the mixture is well molded and firm.

2 Divide the mixture into 16 equal portions. Using your fingers, form each portion into a small round ball.

3 Bring a large pan of water to a boil. Arrange the meatballs on a layer of baking parchment in a steamer and place over the boiling water. Cover and steam for 10 minutes until cooked through.

4 Meanwhile, wash and thinly slice the kumquats. Place them in a pan with the sugar and water and bring to a boil. Simmer for 2–3 minutes until tender.

5 Blend the sherry and cornstarch together and add to the pan. Heat through, stirring, until the kumquat sauce thickens. Season to taste.

6 Drain the meatballs and transfer to a serving plate. Spoon over the sauce and serve with pasta and vegetables.

Chicken & Spinach Lasagna

A delicious pasta bake with all the colors of the Italian flag—red tomatoes, green spinach and pasta, and white chicken and sauce.

NUTRITIONAL INFORMATION

Calories 358	Sugars 12g
Protein 42g	Fat 9g
Carbohydrate ..22g	Saturates 4g

🧀 🧀 🧀

🥣 25 mins   🕐 50 mins

SERVES 4

INGREDIENTS

12 oz/350 g frozen chopped spinach, thawed and drained

½ tsp ground nutmeg

1 lb/450 g lean, cooked chicken meat, skinned and diced

4 sheets pre-cooked lasagna verde

1½ tbsp cornstarch

1¾ cups skim milk

¾ cup freshly grated Parmesan cheese

TOMATO SAUCE

14 oz/400 g canned chopped tomatoes

1 onion, finely chopped

1 garlic clove, crushed

⅔ cup white wine

3 tbsp tomato paste

1 tsp dried oregano

salt and pepper

salad greens, to serve

2 Drain the spinach again and spread it out on paper towels to make sure that as much water as possible is removed. Layer the spinach in the bottom of an ovenproof baking dish. Sprinkle with nutmeg and season to taste.

3 Arrange the diced chicken over the spinach and spoon over the tomato sauce. Arrange the sheets of lasagna over the tomato sauce layer.

4 Blend the cornstarch into a paste with a little of the milk. Pour the remaining milk into a pan and stir in the cornstarch paste. Heat for 2–3 minutes, stirring, until the sauce thickens. Season well.

5 Spoon the sauce over the lasagna and transfer the dish to a cookie sheet. Sprinkle the grated cheese over the sauce and bake in the oven for 25 minutes until golden brown. Serve with salad greens.

1 Preheat the oven to 400°F/200°C. For the tomato sauce, place the tomatoes in a pan and stir in the onion, garlic, wine, tomato paste, and oregano. Bring to a boil and simmer for 20 minutes until thick. Season well and keep warm.

Chicken & Tomato Lasagna

This variation of the traditional beef dish has layers of pasta, and chicken or turkey, baked in red wine, tomatoes, and a delicious cheese sauce.

NUTRITIONAL INFORMATION

Calories 550	Sugars 11g
Protein 35g	Fat 29g
Carbohydrate . . 34g	Saturates 12g

🍞 🍞 🍞

🍲 20 mins 🕐 1¼ hrs

SERVES 4

INGREDIENTS

12 oz/350 g fresh lasagna or 5½ oz/150 g dried lasagna (about 9 sheets)

butter, for greasing

1 tbsp olive oil

1 red onion, finely chopped

1 garlic clove, crushed

3½ oz/100 g mushrooms, wiped and sliced

12 oz/350 g chicken or turkey breast, cut into chunks

⅔ cup red wine, diluted with scant ⅓ cup water

9 oz/250 g strained tomatoes

1 tsp sugar

BECHAMEL SAUCE

5 tbsp butter

6 tbsp all-purpose flour

2½ cups milk

1 egg, beaten

generous ¾ cup freshly grated Parmesan cheese

salt and pepper

1 Cook the lasagna according to the instructions on the packet. Lightly grease a deep ovenproof dish.

2 Heat the oil in a pan. Add the onion and garlic and cook for 3–4 minutes. Add the mushrooms and chicken and stir-fry for 4 minutes or until the meat browns.

3 Add the wine, bring to a boil, then simmer for 5 minutes. Stir in the strained tomatoes and sugar, and cook for 3–5 minutes until the meat is tender and cooked through. The sauce should be thick, but quite runny.

4 To make the Béchamel Sauce, melt the butter in a pan, stir in the flour, and cook for 2 minutes. Remove the pan from the heat and gradually add the milk, mixing to form a smooth sauce. Return the pan to the heat and bring to a boil, stirring until thickened. Let cool slightly, then beat in the egg and half of the cheese. Season to taste.

5 Place 3 sheets of lasagna in the bottom of the dish and spread with half of the chicken mixture. Repeat the layers. Top with the last 3 sheets of lasagna, pour over the Béchamel Sauce, and sprinkle with the Parmesan cheese. Bake in a preheated oven, at 375°F/190°C, for 30 minutes until golden and the pasta is cooked.

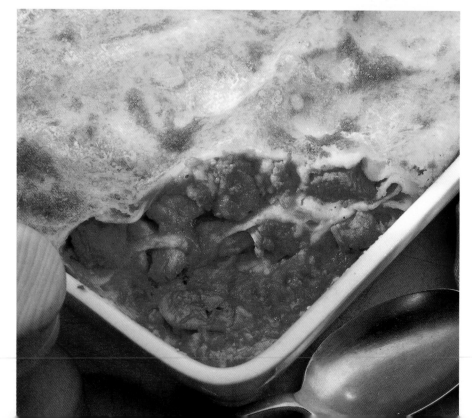

Smoked Haddock Casserole

This quick, easy, and inexpensive dish would be ideal for a midweek family supper.

NUTRITIONAL INFORMATION

Calories 525   Sugars 8g
Protein ....41g   Fat 18g
Carbohydrate ...53g   Saturates 10g

20 mins | 45 mins

SERVES 4

INGREDIENTS

2 tbsp butter, plus extra for greasing

1 lb/450 g smoked haddock fillets, cut into 4 slices

2½ cups milk

2 tbsp all-purpose flour

pinch of freshly grated nutmeg

3 tbsp heavy cream

1 tbsp chopped fresh parsley

2 eggs, hard-cooked and mashed to a pulp

1 lb/450 g dried fusilli

1 tbsp lemon juice

salt and pepper

boiled new potatoes and beets, to serve

1 Thoroughly grease a casserole with butter. Put the haddock in the casserole and pour over the milk. Bake in a preheated oven, 400°F/200°C, for about 15 minutes. Carefully pour the cooking liquid into a pitcher without breaking up the fish.

2 Melt the 2 tablespoons of butter in a pan and stir in the flour. Gradually whisk in the reserved cooking liquid. Season to taste, with salt, pepper, and nutmeg. Stir in the cream, parsley, and mashed egg and cook, stirring constantly, for 2 minutes.

3 Meanwhile, bring a large pan of lightly salted water to a boil. Add the fusilli and lemon juice and cook for 8–10 minutes until tender, but still firm to the bite.

4 Drain the pasta, and spoon or tip it over the fish. Top with the egg sauce and return the casserole to the oven for another 10 minutes.

5 Serve the fish casserole with boiled new potatoes and freshly cooked beets.

VARIATION

You can use any type of dried pasta for this casserole. Try penne, conchiglie, or rigatoni.

Sea Bass with Olive Sauce

A favorite fish for chefs, the delicious sea bass is now becoming increasingly common in large food stores and fish stores for family meals.

NUTRITIONAL INFORMATION

Calories	877	Sugars	3g
Protein	50g	Fat	47g
Carbohydrate	67g	Saturates	26g

🦪 10 mins   🕐 30 mins

SERVES 4

I N G R E D I E N T S

1 lb/450 g dried macaroni

1 tbsp olive oil

8 x 4 oz/115 g sea bass medallions

S A U C E

2 tbsp butter

4 shallots, chopped

2 tbsp capers

1½ cups chopped pitted green olives

4 tbsp balsamic vinegar

1¼ cups fish bouillon

1¼ cups heavy cream

juice of 1 lemon

salt and pepper

T O   G A R N I S H

lemon slices

shredded leek

shredded carrot

1 To make the sauce, melt the butter in a skillet. Add the shallots and cook gently over a low heat for 4 minutes. Add the capers and chopped olives and cook for a further 3 minutes.

2 Stir in the balsamic vinegar and fish bouillon, bring to a boil and reduce by half. Add the cream, stirring, and reduce again by half. Season to taste with salt and pepper and stir in the lemon juice. Remove the pan from the heat, set aside and keep warm.

3 Bring a large pan of lightly salted water to a boil. Add the pasta and olive oil and cook for about 12 minutes, or until tender, but still firm to the bite.

4 Meanwhile, lightly broil the sea bass medallions for 3–4 minutes on each side, until cooked through, but still moist and delicate.

5 Drain the pasta thoroughly and transfer to large individual serving dishes. Top the pasta with the fish medallions and pour over the olive sauce. Garnish the sea bass with lemon slices, shredded leek, and shredded carrot, and serve immediately.

Spaghetti alla Bucaniera

A combination of hard cider and tarragon vinegar gives mouthwatering flavor to this warming dish.

NUTRITIONAL INFORMATION

Calories	588	Sugars	........5g
Protein	.......36g	Fat	..........18g
Carbohydrate	..68g	Saturates	......9g

25 mins   50 mins

SERVES 4

INGREDIENTS

¾ cup all-purpose flour

1 lb/450 g brill or sole fillets, skinned and chopped

1 lb/450 g hake fillets, skinned and chopped

6 tbsp butter

4 shallots, finely chopped

2 garlic cloves, crushed

1 carrot, diced

1 leek, finely chopped

1¼ cups hard cider

1¼ cups apple juice

2 tsp anchovy paste

1 tbsp tarragon vinegar

1 lb/450 g dried spaghetti

1 tbsp olive oil

salt and pepper

chopped fresh parsley, to garnish

warm crusty brown bread, to serve

1 Season the flour with salt and pepper. Sprinkle ¼ cup of the seasoned flour on to a shallow plate. Press the fish pieces into the seasoned flour to coat thoroughly.

2 Melt the butter in a flameproof casserole. Add the fish fillets, shallots, garlic, carrot, and leek, and cook over a low heat, stirring frequently, for about 10 minutes.

3 Sprinkle over the remaining seasoned flour and cook, stirring constantly, for 2 minutes. Gradually stir in the hard cider, apple juice, anchovy paste, and tarragon vinegar. Bring to a boil and simmer over a low heat for 35 minutes. Alternatively, bake the fish in a preheated oven, 350°F/180°C, for approximately 30 minutes.

4 About 15 minutes before the end of the cooking time, bring a large pan of lightly salted water to a boil. Add the spaghetti and olive oil and cook without a lid for about 12 minutes, or until the pasta is al dente—quite tender, but still firm to the bite. Drain the pasta thoroughly and transfer it to a large serving dish.

5 Arrange the fish on top of the spaghetti and pour over the sauce. Garnish with chopped parsley and serve immediately with warm, crusty brown bread.

Fillets of Red Mullet & Pasta

A lemon and herb sauce perfectly complements the sweet flavor and delicate texture of the fish.

NUTRITIONAL INFORMATION

Calories	 457	Sugars	.... 3g
Protein	.... 39g	Fat	.... 12g
Carbohydrate	.. 44g	Saturates	...... 5g

🥘 🥘 🥘

🧊 15 mins   🕐 1 hr

SERVES 4

INGREDIENTS

2 lb 4 oz/1 kg red mullet fillets

1¼ cups dry white wine

4 shallots, finely chopped

1 garlic clove, crushed

3 tbsp finely chopped mixed fresh herbs

finely grated zest and juice of 1 lemon

pinch of freshly grated nutmeg

3 anchovy fillets, roughly chopped

1 tbsp butter

2 tbsp heavy cream

1 tsp cornstarch

1 lb/450 g dried vermicelli

1 tbsp olive oil

salt and pepper

TO GARNISH

1 fresh mint sprig

lemon slices

lemon zest

1 Put the red mullet fillets in a large casserole. Pour over the wine and add half the chopped shallots with the garlic, herbs, lemon zest and juice, nutmeg, and anchovies. Season, cover the casserole, and bake in a preheated oven, 350°F/180°C, for 35 minutes.

2 Transfer the baked fish carefully to a warm plate. Set the plate aside and keep warm.

3 Heat the butter in a pan and cook the remaining shallots over a low heat, stirring, for 5 minutes. Pour the cooking liquid into the pan and bring to a boil. Simmer for 25 minutes, until reduced by half. Mix the cream and cornstarch and stir into the sauce to thicken.

4 Meanwhile, bring a pan of lightly salted water to a boil. Add the vermicelli and oil and cook for 8–10 minutes, or until tender, but still firm to the bite. Drain the pasta and transfer to a warm serving dish.

5 Arrange the fish fillets on top of the vermicelli and pour over the sauce. Garnish with a fresh mint sprig, slices of lemon, and strips of lemon zest, and serve immediately.

Spaghetti al Tonno

The classic Italian combination of pasta and tuna is enhanced in this recipe with a delicious parsley sauce.

NUTRITIONAL INFORMATION

Calories 1065	Sugars 3g	
Protein 27g	Fat 85g	
Carbohydrate .. 52g	Saturates 18g	

10 mins | 15 mins

SERVES 4

INGREDIENTS

7 oz/200 g canned tuna, drained

2 oz/60 g canned anchovies, drained

1⅛ cup olive oil

1 cup roughly chopped flatleaf parsley

⅔ cup unsweetened yogurt

1 lb/450 g dried spaghetti

2 tbsp butter

salt and pepper

black olives, to garnish

warm crusty bread, to serve

1 Remove any bones from the tuna. Put the tuna into a food processor or blender, together with the anchovies, 1 cup of the olive oil, and the flatleaf parsley. Process until the sauce is very smooth.

2 Spoon the yogurt into the food processor or blender and process again for a few seconds to blend thoroughly. Season with salt and pepper to taste.

3 Bring a large pan of lightly salted water to a boil. Add the spaghetti and the remaining olive oil and cook for 8–10 minutes, or until tender, but still firm to the bite.

4 Drain the spaghetti, return to the pan, and place over a medium heat. Add the butter and toss well to coat. Spoon in the sauce and quickly toss into the spaghetti, mixing well using 2 forks.

5 Remove the pan from the heat and divide the spaghetti between warm individual serving plates. Garnish with olives and serve with warm, crusty bread.

VARIATION

If desired, you could add 1–2 garlic cloves to the sauce, substitute ½ cup chopped fresh basil for half the parsley, and garnish with capers instead of black olives.

Poached Salmon with Penne

Fresh salmon and pasta in a mouthwatering lemon sauce—a wonderful summer evening treat.

NUTRITIONAL INFORMATION

Calories	 968	Sugars	.... 3g
Protein	.... 59g	Fat	.... 58g
Carbohydrate	.. 49g	Saturates	..... 19g

🍳 10 mins   🕐 30 mins

SERVES 4

I N G R E D I E N T S

4 x 9½ oz/275 g fresh salmon steaks

4 tbsp butter

¾ cup dry white wine

sea salt

8 peppercorns

fresh dill sprig

fresh tarragon sprig

1 lemon, sliced

1 lb/450 g dried penne

2 tbsp olive oil

lemon slices and fresh young spinach
   leaves, to garnish

L E M O N   S A U C E

2 tbsp butter

3 tbsp all-purpose flour

⅔ cup warm milk

juice and finely grated zest of 2 lemons

2 oz/60 g watercress or young spinach
   leaves, chopped, plus extra to garnish

salt and pepper

1 Place the salmon in a large, non-stick pan. Add the butter, white wine, a pinch of sea salt, the peppercorns, dill, tarragon, and lemon. Cover, bring to a boil, and simmer for 10 minutes.

2 Using a spatula, carefully remove the salmon. Strain and reserve the cooking liquid. Remove and discard the salmon skin and center bones. Place on a warm dish, cover, and keep warm.

3 Meanwhile, bring a pan of salted water to a boil. Add the penne and 1 tablespoon of the oil and cook for 8–10 minutes, or until tender but still firm to the bite. Drain and sprinkle over the remaining olive oil. Place on a warm serving dish, top with the salmon steaks, and keep warm.

4 To make the sauce, melt the butter and stir in the flour for 2 minutes. Stir in the milk and about 7 tablespoons of the reserved cooking liquid. Add the lemon juice and zest and cook, stirring, for a further 10 minutes.

5 Add the watercress or spinach to the sauce, stir gently, and season to taste with salt and pepper.

6 Pour the sauce over the salmon and penne, garnish with slices of lemon and fresh watercress, and serve.

Trout with Smoked Bacon

Most trout available nowadays is farmed rainbow trout. However, if you can, buy wild brown trout for this recipe.

NUTRITIONAL INFORMATION

Calories 802   Sugars 8g
Protein .... 68g   Fat 36g
Carbohydrate .. 54g   Saturates 10g

35 mins   25 mins

SERVES 4

INGREDIENTS

butter, for greasing

4 x 9½ oz/275 g trout, gutted and cleaned

12 anchovies in oil, drained and chopped

2 apples, peeled, cored, and sliced

4 fresh mint sprigs

juice of 1 lemon

12 slices rindless smoked fatty bacon

1 lb/450 g dried tagliatelle

1 tbsp olive oil

salt and pepper

TO GARNISH

2 apples, cored and sliced

4 fresh mint sprigs

1 Grease a deep cookie sheet with plenty of butter. Set aside.

2 Open up the cavities of each trout and rinse with warm salt water.

3 Season each cavity with salt and pepper. Divide the anchovies, sliced apples, and mint sprigs between each of the cavities. Sprinkle the lemon juice into each cavity.

4 Carefully cover the whole of each trout, except the head and tail, with three strips of smoked bacon in a spiral.

5 Arrange the trout on the cookie sheet with the loose ends of the bacon strips tucked underneath. Season the fish with pepper and bake in a preheated oven, 400°F/200°C, for 20 minutes, turning the trout over after the first 10 minutes.

6 Meanwhile, bring a large pan of lightly salted water to a boil. Add the tagliatelle and olive oil and cook for about 12 minutes, or until tender, but still firm to the bite. Drain the pasta and transfer to a large, warm serving dish.

7 Remove the trout from the oven and arrange on the tagliatelle. Garnish with apple slices and mint to serve.

Seafood Lasagna

You can use any fish and any sauce you like in this recipe: try smoked haddock and whiskey sauce, or cod with cheese sauce.

NUTRITIONAL INFORMATION

Calories 790   Sugars 23g
Protein .... 55g   Fat 32g
Carbohydrate .. 74g   Saturates 19g

30 mins   45 mins

SERVES 4

INGREDIENTS

1 lb/450 g smoked haddock, filleted, skin removed, and flesh flaked

4 oz/115 g shrimp

4 oz/115 g sole fillet, skin removed and flesh sliced

juice of 1 lemon

SAUCE

4 tbsp butter

3 leeks, very thinly sliced

½ cup all-purpose flour

2 cups milk

2 tbsp clear honey

1¾ cups grated mozzarella cheese

1 lb/450 g pre-cooked lasagna

⅔ cup freshly grated Parmesan cheese

pepper

VARIATION

For a cider sauce, substitute 1 finely chopped shallot for the leeks, 1½ cups hard cider and 1½ cups heavy cream for the milk, and 1 teaspoon of mustard for the honey. For a Tuscan sauce, substitute 1 chopped fennel bulb for the leeks; omit the honey.

1 Put the haddock fillet, shrimp, and sole fillet into a large bowl and season with pepper and lemon juice, according to taste. Cover the bowl and set it aside while you make the sauce.

2 Melt the butter in a large pan. Add the leeks and cook, stirring occasionally, for 8 minutes. Add the flour and cook, stirring constantly, for 1 minute. Gradually stir in enough milk to make a thick, creamy sauce.

3 Blend in the honey and mozzarella cheese and continue cooking for a further 3 minutes. Remove the pan from the heat and mix in the fish and shrimp.

4 Make alternate layers of fish sauce and lasagna in an ovenproof dish, finishing with a fish sauce layer on top. Generously sprinkle over the grated Parmesan cheese and bake in a preheated oven, 350°F/180°C, for 30 minutes. Serve immediately.

Pasta & Shrimp Parcels

This is the ideal dish when you have unexpected guests because the parcels are quick to prepare but look fantastic.

NUTRITIONAL INFORMATION

Calories	640	Sugars	1g
Protein	50g	Fat	29g
Carbohydrate	42g	Saturates	4g

🄖 🄖 🄖

🍴 15 mins   🕐 30 mins

SERVES 4

INGREDIENTS

1 lb/450 g dried fettuccine

⅔ cup Pesto Sauce (see page 73)

4 tsp extra virgin olive oil

1 lb 10 oz/750 g large raw shrimp, peeled and deveined

2 garlic cloves, crushed

½ cup dry white wine

salt and pepper

3 Mix together the fettuccine and half of the Pesto Sauce. Spread out the paper squares and put 1 teaspoon of olive oil in the middle of each. Divide the fettuccine between the the squares, then divide the shrimp and place on top of the fettuccine.

4 Mix together the remaining Pesto Sauce and the garlic and spoon it over the shrimp. Season each parcel with salt and pepper and sprinkle with the wine.

5 Dampen the edges of the waxed paper and wrap the parcels loosely, twisting the edges to seal.

6 Place the parcels on a cookie sheet and bake in a preheated oven, 400°F/200°C, for 10–15 minutes. Transfer the parcels to individual serving plates and serve.

1 Cut out four 12 inch/30 cm squares of waxed paper.

2 Bring a large pan of lightly salted water to a boil. Add the fettuccine and cook for 2–3 minutes, until just softened. Drain and set aside.

COOK'S TIP

Traditionally, these parcels are designed to look like money bags. The resemblance is more effective with waxed paper than with foil.

Vermicelli with Clams

A quickly cooked recipe that transforms ordinary pantry ingredients into a dish with style.

NUTRITIONAL INFORMATION

Calories	520	Sugars	2g
Protein	26g	Fat	13g
Carbohydrate	71g	Saturates	4g

🥄 10 mins 🕐 25 mins

SERVES 4

INGREDIENTS

14 oz/400 g dried vermicelli, spaghetti, or other long pasta

2 tbsp olive oil

2 tbsp butter

2 onions, chopped

2 garlic cloves, chopped

2 x 7 oz/200 g jars clams in brine

½ cup white wine

4 tbsp chopped fresh parsley

½ tsp dried oregano

pinch of freshly grated nutmeg

2 tbsp Parmesan cheese shavings

salt and pepper

fresh basil sprigs, to garnish

1 Bring a large pan of lightly salted water to a boil. Add the pasta and half of the olive oil and cook for 8–10 minutes, or until tender, but still firm to the bite. Drain, return to the pan and add the butter. Cover the pan, shake well and keep warm.

2 Heat the remaining oil in a pan over a medium heat. Add the onions and cook until they are translucent. Stir in the garlic and cook for 1 minute.

3 Strain and reserve the liquid from 1 jar of clams. Add the liquid to the pan, with the wine. Stir, bring to simmering point and simmer for 3 minutes. Drain the second jar of clams and discard the liquid.

4 Add the clams, parsley, and oregano to the pan and season with pepper and nutmeg. Lower the heat and cook until the sauce is heated through.

5 Transfer the pasta to a warm serving dish and pour over the sauce. Sprinkle with the Parmesan cheese shavings, garnish with the basil, and serve immediately.

COOK'S TIP

There are many different types of clams found along almost every coast in the world. Those traditionally used in this dish are the tiny ones, only 1–2 inches/2.5–5 cm across, known in Italy as vongole.

Broccoli & Anchovy Pasta

Orecchiette, the cup-shaped pasta from southern Italy, is excellent for this filling dish because it scoops up the robust, chunky sauce.

NUTRITIONAL INFORMATION

Calories	 685	Sugars	.... 4g
Protein	.... 33g	Fat	.... 29g
Carbohydrate	.. 78g	Saturates	...... 9g

🥶 5 mins 🕐 25 mins

SERVES 4

INGREDIENTS

1 lb 2 oz/500 g broccoli

14 oz/400 g dried orecchiette

5 tbsp olive oil

2 large garlic cloves, crushed

1¾ oz/50 g canned anchovy fillets in oil, drained and finely chopped

2 oz/60 g Parmesan cheese, grated

2 oz/60 g romano cheese, grated

salt and pepper

1 Bring 2 pans of lightly salted water to a boil. Chop the broccoli florets and stems into small, bite-sized pieces. Add the broccoli to one pan and cook until very tender. Drain and set aside.

2 Put the pasta in the other pan of boiling water and cook for 10–12 minutes, or according to the packet instructions until tender, but still al dente.

3 Meanwhile, heat the olive oil in a large pan over a medium heat. Add the garlic and cook for 3 minutes, stirring, without allowing it to brown. Add the chopped anchovies and cook for 3 minutes, stirring and mashing with a wooden spoon.

4 Drain the pasta, add to the pan of anchovies and stir. Add the broccoli and stir to mix.

5 Add the grated Parmesan and romano to the pasta and stir constantly over a medium-high heat until the cheeses melt and the pasta and broccoli are coated.

6 Adjust the seasoning to taste—the anchovies and cheeses are salty, so you will only need to add pepper, if anything. Spoon into individual bowls or on to plates and serve immediately.

VARIATIONS

Add dried chili flakes to taste with the garlic in step 3, if desired. If you have difficulty in finding orecchiette, try using conchiglie instead.

Pasta with Tuna & Lemon

Fusilli—corkscrew-shape pasta—is the best shape to use for this recipe because the creamy sauce is absorbed in the twists.

NUTRITIONAL INFORMATION

Calories 891	Sugars 6g
Protein 27g	Fat 55g
Carbohydrate .. 77g	Saturates 31g

5 mins

15 mins

SERVES 4

I N G R E D I E N T S

4 tbsp butter, diced

1¼ cups heavy cream

4 tbsp lemon juice

1 tbsp grated lemon zest

½ tsp anchovy paste

14 oz/400 g dried fusilli

7 oz/200 g canned tuna in olive oil, drained and flaked

salt and pepper

T O   G A R N I S H

2 tbsp finely chopped fresh parsley

strips of lemon zest

1 Bring a large pan of lightly salted water to a boil. Melt the butter in a large skillet. Stir in the heavy cream and lemon juice and let simmer, stirring, for about 2 minutes, until slightly thickened.

2 Stir in the lemon zest and anchovy paste. Meanwhile, cook the pasta for 10–12 minutes, or according to the instructions on the packet, until tender, but still firm to the bite. Drain well.

3 Add the sauce to the pasta and toss until well coated. Add the tuna and gently toss until well blended but without breaking up the tuna.

4 Season to taste with salt and pepper. Transfer to a serving platter and garnish with the parsley and lemon zest. Grind over some pepper and serve at once.

VARIATIONS

For a vegetarian version, omit the tuna and anchovy paste. Add 5 oz/150 g pitted olives instead. For extra "kick" add a pinch of dried chili flakes to the sauce instead of the anchovy paste.

Sicilian Tagliatelle

This is based on a Sicilian dish combining broccoli and anchovies, but I have added lemon and garlic for more flavor.

NUTRITIONAL INFORMATION

Calories	529	Sugars	........4g
Protein	.......17g	Fat	..........20g
Carbohydrate	..75g	Saturates	......3g

5 mins

10–15 mins

SERVES 4

INGREDIENTS

6 tbsp olive oil

4 tbsp fresh white breadcrumbs

1 lb/450 g broccoli, cut into small florets

12 oz/350 g dried tagliatelle

4 anchovy fillets, drained and chopped

2 garlic cloves, sliced

grated zest 1 lemon

large pinch of chili flakes

salt and pepper

freshly grated Parmesan cheese, to serve

1 Heat 2 tablespoons of the olive oil in a skillet and add the breadcrumbs. Cook over a medium heat for 4–5 minutes until golden and crisp. Remove from the pan and drain on paper towels.

2 Bring a large pan of salted water to a boil and add the broccoli. Blanch for 3 minutes then drain, reserving the water. Refresh the broccoli under cold water and drain again. Set the florets aside to dry on paper towels.

3 Bring the water back to a boil and add the tagliatelle. Cook according to the packet instructions, until tender, but still firm to the bite.

4 Meanwhile, heat another 2 tablespoons of the olive oil in a large skillet or wok and add the chopped anchovies. Cook for 1 minute then mash with a wooden spoon to a paste. Add the garlic, lemon zest, and chili flakes, and cook gently for 2 minutes. Add the broccoli and cook for a further 3–4 minutes until heated through.

5 Drain the pasta and add to the broccoli mixture with the rest of the olive oil and seasoning. Toss together well.

6 Divide the pasta between individual serving plates. Top with the sautéed breadcrumbs and grated Parmesan cheese and serve immediately.

Linguine with Sardines

This is a very quick dish that is ideal for mid-week suppers as it is so simple to prepare but full of flavor.

NUTRITIONAL INFORMATION

Calories 547	Sugars 5g
Protein 23g	Fat 23g
Carbohydrate . . 68g	Saturates 3g

5–10 mins   10–15 mins

SERVES 4

INGREDIENTS

8 sardines, filleted

1 fennel bulb

4 tbsp olive oil

3 garlic cloves, sliced

1 tsp chili flakes

12 oz/350 g dried linguine

½ tsp finely grated lemon zest

1 tbsp lemon juice

2 tbsp pine nuts, toasted

2 tbsp chopped fresh parsley, plus extra for garnish

salt and pepper

1 Wash and dry the sardines. Roughly chop them into large pieces and set aside. Trim the fennel bulb, removing any tough outer leaves, and slice very thinly.

2 Heat 2 tablespoons of the olive oil in a large skillet and add the garlic and chili flakes. Cook for 1 minute then add the fennel. Cook over a medium-high heat for 4–5 minutes until softened. Add the sardine pieces and heat for a further 3–4 minutes until just cooked.

3 Meanwhile, cook the pasta in plenty of boiling salted water according to the packet instructions, until tender, but still firm to the bite. Drain well and return to the pan to keep warm.

4 Add the lemon zest and juice, pine nuts, parsley, and seasoning to the sardines and toss together. Add to the pasta with the remaining olive oil and toss together gently. Serve immediately with a sprinkling of parsley.

COOK'S TIP

Reserve a couple of tablespoons of the pasta cooking water and add to the pasta with the sauce if the mixture seems a little dry.

Spaghettini with Crab

This dish is probably one of the simplest in the book, yet the flavor is as impressive as a recipe over which you have slaved for hours.

NUTRITIONAL INFORMATION

Calories 488	Sugars 3g	
Protein 13g	Fat 19g	
Carbohydrate .. 65g	Saturates 3g	

5 mins   5 mins

SERVES 4

I N G R E D I E N T S

1 dressed crab, about 1 lb/450 g including the shell

12 oz/350 g dried spaghettini

6 tbsp best quality extra virgin olive oil

1 hot red chile, deseeded and finely chopped

2 garlic cloves, finely chopped

3 tbsp chopped fresh parsley

1 tsp finely grated lemon zest

2 tbsp lemon juice

salt and pepper

lemon wedges, to garnish

1 Scoop the meat from the crab shell into a bowl. Mix the white and brown meat lightly together and set aside.

2 Bring a large pan of salted water to a boil and add the spaghettini. Cook according to the instructions on the packet, until tender, but still firm to the bite. Drain well and return to the pan.

3 Meanwhile, heat 2 tablespoons of the olive oil in a skillet. When hot, add the chile and garlic. Cook for 30 seconds before adding the crab meat, parsley, lemon zest and juice. Stir-fry for a further minute until the crab is just heated through.

4 Add the crab mixture to the pasta with the remaining olive oil, season to taste, and toss together well. Serve immediately, garnished with lemon wedges.

Vegetables & Bean Curd

This is a simple, clean-tasting dish of green vegetables, bean curd, and pasta, lightly tossed in olive oil.

NUTRITIONAL INFORMATION

Calories	400	Sugars	5g
Protein	19g	Fat	17g
Carbohydrate	46g	Saturates	5g

25 mins

20 mins

SERVES 4

INGREDIENTS

8 oz/225 g asparagus

4½ oz/125 g snow peas

8 oz/225 g green beans

1 leek

8 oz/225 g shelled small fava beans

10½ oz/300 g dried fusilli

2 tbsp olive oil

2 tbsp butter or margarine

1 garlic clove, crushed

8 oz/225 g bean curd, cut into
    1 inch/2.5 cm cubes

⅓ cup pitted green olives in brine, drained

salt and pepper

freshly grated Parmesan, to serve

3 Bring a large pan of salted water to a boil. Cook the fusilli for 8–9 minutes until just tender. Drain thoroughly. Toss in 1 tablespoon of the oil and season well.

4 Meanwhile, in a wok or large skillet, heat the remaining oil and the butter or margarine and gently cook the leek, garlic and bean curd for 1–2 minutes, until the vegetables have just softened.

5 Stir in the snow peas and continue cooking for 1 minute.

6 Add the boiled vegetables and olives to the skillet and heat through for just 1 minute. Carefully stir in the pasta and add seasoning. Cook for an additional minute and then pile into a warmed serving dish. Serve while still hot, sprinkled with grated Parmesan cheese.

1 Cut the asparagus into 2 inch/5 cm lengths. Finely slice the snow peas diagonally and slice the green beans into 1 inch/2.5 cm pieces. Finely slice the leek.

2 Bring a large pan of water to a boil and add the asparagus, green beans, and fava beans. Bring back to a boil and cook for 4 minutes until just tender. Drain well and rinse in cold water. Set aside.

Pasta with Nuts & Cheese

Simple and inexpensive, this tasty and nutritious pasta dish can be prepared fairly quickly.

NUTRITIONAL INFORMATION

Calories	750	Sugars	6g
Protein	23g	Fat	44g
Carbohydrate	70g	Saturates	21g

🕐 10 mins   ⏱ 30 mins

SERVES 4

I N G R E D I E N T S

1 cup pine nuts

12 oz/350 g dried pasta shapes

2 zucchini, sliced

1¼ cups broccoli florets

1 cup full-fat soft cheese

⅔ cup milk

1 tbsp chopped fresh basil

4½ oz/125 g white mushrooms, sliced

3 oz/90 g blue cheese, crumbled

salt and pepper

sprigs of fresh basil, to garnish

salad greens, to serve

1 Scatter the pine nuts on to a cookie sheet and broil, turning occasionally, until lightly browned all over. Set aside.

2 Cook the pasta in plenty of boiling salted water for 8–10 minutes, or until just tender, but still firm to the bite.

3 Meanwhile, cook the zucchini and broccoli in a small amount of boiling, lightly salted water for about 5 minutes or until they are just tender.

4 Put the soft cheese into a pan and heat gently, stirring. Add the milk and stir to mix. Add the basil and mushrooms and cook gently for 2–3 minutes. Stir in the blue cheese and season to taste.

5 Drain the pasta and the vegetables and mix together. Pour over the cheese and mushroom sauce and add the pine nuts. Toss gently to mix. Garnish with basil sprigs and serve with salad greens.

Pasta Provençale

A Mediterranean mixture of red bell peppers, garlic, and zucchini, cooked in olive oil and tossed with pasta spirals.

NUTRITIONAL INFORMATION

Calories 487	Sugars 14g
Protein 17g	Fat 24g
Carbohydrate .. 53g	Saturates 8g

5 mins 20 mins

SERVES 4

INGREDIENTS

3 tbsp olive oil

1 onion, sliced

2 garlic cloves, chopped

3 red bell peppers, deseeded and cut into strips

3 zucchini, sliced

14 oz/400 g canned chopped tomatoes

3 tbsp sun-dried tomato paste

2 tbsp chopped fresh basil

8 oz/225 g fresh fusilli

1 cup grated Swiss cheese

salt and pepper

fresh basil sprigs, to garnish

1 Heat the oil in a heavy-based pan or flameproof casserole. Add the onion and garlic and cook, stirring occasionally, until softened. Add the bell peppers and zucchini and cook, stirring occasionally, for 5 minutes.

2 Add the tomatoes, sun-dried tomato paste, and basil, and season to taste with salt and pepper. Cover and cook for a further 5 minutes.

3 Meanwhile, bring a large pan of salted water to a boil and add the pasta. Stir and bring back to a boil. Reduce the heat slightly and cook, uncovered, for 3 minutes, until just tender. Drain the pasta thoroughly and add to the vegetable mixture. Toss gently to mix well.

4 Transfer to a shallow flameproof dish and sprinkle with the cheese.

5 Cook under a preheated broiler for 5 minutes, until the cheese is golden brown and bubbling. Garnish with basil sprigs and serve immediately.

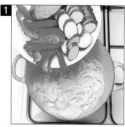

Vegetable Pasta Nests

These large pasta nests look impressive when presented filled with broiled mixed vegetables, and taste delicious.

NUTRITIONAL INFORMATION

Calories ...... 392 Sugars 1g
Protein .... 6g Fat 28g
Carbohydrate .. 32g Saturates 9g

25 mins   40 mins

SERVES 4

INGREDIENTS

6 oz/175 g spaghetti

1 eggplant, halved and sliced

1 zucchini, diced

1 red bell pepper, deseeded and chopped diagonally

6 tbsp olive oil

2 garlic cloves, crushed

4 tbsp butter or margarine, melted

1 tbsp dry white breadcrumbs

salt and pepper

fresh parsley sprigs, to garnish

1 Bring a large pan of water to a boil and cook the spaghetti for 8–10 minutes, or until tender, but still firm to the bite. Drain the spaghetti and set aside until required.

2 Place the eggplant, zucchini, and bell pepper on a cookie sheet. Mix the oil and garlic together and pour over the vegetables, tossing to coat all over.

3 Cook the vegetables under a preheated hot broiler for about 10 minutes, turning, until tender and lightly charred. Set aside and keep warm.

4 Divide the spaghetti among 4 large, lightly greased muffin pans. Using 2 forks, curl the spaghetti to form nests.

5 Brush the pasta nests with melted butter or margarine and sprinkle with the breadcrumbs. Bake in a preheated oven, 400°F/200°C, for 15 minutes or until lightly golden. Remove the pasta nests from the pans and transfer to serving plates. Divide the broiled vegetables between the nests, season, and garnish with parsley sprigs.

Basil & Tomato Pasta

Roasting the tomatoes gives a sweeter flavor to this sauce. Buy Italian tomatoes, such as plum or flavia, as these have a better flavor and color.

NUTRITIONAL INFORMATION

Calories 177	Sugars 4g
Protein 5g	Fat 4g
Carbohydrate .. 31g	Saturates 1g

15 mins   35 mins

SERVES 4

INGREDIENTS

1 tbsp olive oil

2 rosemary sprigs

2 garlic cloves

1 lb/450 g tomatoes, halved

1 tbsp sun-dried tomato paste

12 fresh basil leaves, plus extra to garnish

salt and pepper

1½ lb/675 g fresh farfalle or 12 oz/350 g dried farfalle

1 Place the oil, rosemary, garlic, and tomatoes, skin side up, in a shallow roasting pan.

2 Drizzle with a little olive oil and cook under a preheated broiler for 20 minutes, or until the tomato skins become slightly charred.

3 Peel the skin from the tomatoes. Roughly chop the tomato flesh and place in a pan.

4 Squeeze the pulp from the garlic cloves and mix with the tomato flesh and sun-dried tomato paste.

5 Roughly tear the fresh basil leaves into smaller pieces, then stir them into the sauce. Season with a little salt and pepper to taste. Set aside.

6 Cook the farfalle in a pan of boiling water for 8–10 minutes, or until tender, but still firm to the bite. Drain thoroughly.

7 Gently reheat the tomato and basil sauce, stirring constantly. Take care not to overheat.

8 Transfer the farfalle to serving plates and pour over the basil and tomato sauce. Serve immediately.

COOK'S TIP

This sauce tastes just as good when served cold in a pasta salad.

Spinach & Nut Pasta

Use any pasta shapes that you have for this recipe. Multi-colored tricolor pasta is visually the most attractive.

NUTRITIONAL INFORMATION

Calories ...... 603 Sugars 5g
Protein .... 12g Fat 41g
Carbohydrate .. 46g Saturates 6g

🔥 5 mins   🕐 15 mins

SERVES 4

INGREDIENTS

8 oz/225 g dried pasta shapes

½ cup olive oil

2 garlic cloves, crushed

1 onion, quartered and sliced

3 large flat mushrooms, sliced

8 oz/225 g spinach

2 tbsp pine nuts

6 tbsp dry white wine

salt and pepper

Parmesan shavings, to garnish

3 Add the sliced mushrooms to the pan and cook over a medium heat, stirring occasionally, for 2 minutes.

4 Lower the heat, add the spinach to the pan and cook, stirring occasionally, for 4–5 minutes, or until it has wilted.

5 Stir in the pine nuts and wine, season to taste, and cook for 1 minute.

6 Transfer the pasta to a warm serving bowl and toss the sauce into it, mixing well. Garnish with shavings of Parmesan cheese and serve.

1 Cook the pasta in a pan of boiling salted water for 8–10 minutes, or until tender, but still firm to the bite. Drain well.

2 Meanwhile, heat the oil in a large pan and cook the crushed garlic and onion for 1 minute.

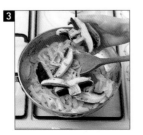

COOK'S TIP
Grate a little nutmeg over the dish for extra flavor, as this spice has a particular affinity with spinach.

Macaroni Cheese & Tomato

This is a really simple, family dish which is inexpensive and easy to prepare and cook. Serve with a salad or fresh green vegetables.

NUTRITIONAL INFORMATION

Calories	 592	Sugars	. . . . 6g
Protein	. . . . 28g	Fat	. . . . 29g
Carbohydrate	. . 57g	Saturates	. . . . . 17g

🄖 🄖 🄖

15 mins | 35–40 mins

SERVES 4

I N G R E D I E N T S

8 oz/225 g dried elbow macaroni

1½ cups grated Cheddar cheese

1 cup freshly grated Parmesan cheese

4 tbsp fresh white breadcrumbs

1 tbsp chopped basil

1 tbsp butter or margarine, plus extra for greasing

T O M A T O   S A U C E

1 tbsp olive oil

1 shallot, finely chopped

2 garlic cloves, crushed

1 lb 2 oz/500 g canned chopped tomatoes

1 tbsp chopped basil

salt and pepper

1 To make the tomato sauce, heat the oil in a heavy-based pan. Add the shallot and garlic and cook for 1 minute. Add the tomatoes and basil, and season with salt and pepper to taste. Cook over a medium heat, stirring constantly, for 10 minutes.

2 Meanwhile, bring a large pan of lightly salted water to a boil and cook the macaroni for 8 minutes, or until tender, but still firm to the bite. Drain thoroughly and set aside.

3 Mix the Cheddar and Parmesan together in a bowl. Grease a deep, ovenproof dish. Spoon one-third of the tomato sauce into the bottom of the dish, top with one-third of the macaroni and then one-third of the cheeses. Season to taste with salt and pepper. Repeat these layers twice, ending with a layer of grated cheese.

4 Combine the breadcrumbs and chopped basil and sprinkle evenly over the top. Dot the topping with butter or margarine and cook in a preheated oven, 375°F/190°C, for 25 minutes, or until the the topping is golden brown and bubbling. Serve immediately.

Tagliarini with Gorgonzola

This simple, creamy pasta sauce is a classic Italian recipe. You could use Danish blue cheese instead of the Gorgonzola, if you prefer.

NUTRITIONAL INFORMATION

Calories 904	Sugars 4g	
Protein 27g	Fat 53g	
Carbohydrate ... 83g	Saturates 36g	

5 mins　　　　20 mins

SERVES 4

INGREDIENTS

2 tbsp butter

2½ cups Gorgonzola cheese, coarsely crumbled

scant ⅔ cup heavy cream

2 tbsp dry white wine

1 tsp cornstarch

4 fresh sage sprigs, finely chopped

14 oz/400 g dried tagliarini

2 tbsp olive oil

salt and white pepper

1 Melt the butter in a heavy-based pan. Stir in 2 cups of the cheese and melt, over a low heat, for about 2 minutes.

2 Add the cream, wine, and cornstarch and beat with a whisk until the ingredients are fully incorporated.

3 Stir in the sage and season to taste with salt and white pepper. Bring to a boil over a low heat, whisking constantly, until the sauce thickens. Remove from the heat and set aside while you cook the pasta.

4 Bring a large pan of lightly salted water to a boil. Add the tagliarini and 1 tablespoon of the olive oil. Cook the pasta for 8–10 minutes or until just tender, drain thoroughly, and toss in the remaining olive oil. Transfer the pasta to a serving dish and keep warm.

5 Reheat the sauce over a low heat, whisking constantly. Spoon the Gorgonzola sauce over the tagliarini, generously sprinkle over the remaining cheese, and serve immediately.

COOK'S TIP

Gorgonzola is one of the world's oldest veined cheeses and, arguably, its finest. When buying, always check that it is creamy yellow with delicate green veining. Avoid hard or discolored cheese. It should have a rich, piquant aroma, not a bitter smell.

Three Cheese Bake

Serve this dish while the cheese is still hot and melted, as cooked cheese turns very rubbery if it is allowed to cool down.

NUTRITIONAL INFORMATION

Calories 710	Sugars 6g
Protein 34g	Fat 30g
Carbohydrate . . 80g	Saturates 16g

5 mins   1 hr

SERVES 4

I N G R E D I E N T S

butter, for greasing

14 oz/400 g dried penne pasta

1 tbsp olive oil

2 eggs, beaten

12 oz/350 g ricotta cheese

4 sprigs fresh basil

3½ oz/100 g mozzarella or halloumi cheese, grated

¾ cup freshly grated Parmesan cheese

salt and pepper

fresh basil leaves, to garnish (optional)

1 Lightly grease a large ovenproof dish with butter and set it aside.

2 Bring a large pan of lightly salted water to a boil. Add the penne and olive oil and cook for 8–10 minutes, or until just tender, but still firm to the bite. Drain the pasta, set aside and keep warm.

3 Break the eggs into a bowl and beat lightly together, then beat the eggs into the ricotta cheese and season the mixture to taste.

4 Spoon half of the penne into the bottom of the prepared dish and cover with half of the basil leaves.

5 Spoon over half of the ricotta cheese mixture. Sprinkle over the mozzarella or halloumi cheese and top with the remaining basil leaves. Cover with the remaining penne, then spoon over the remaining ricotta cheese mixture. Lightly sprinkle the grated Parmesan cheese over the top.

6 Bake in a preheated oven, 375°F/190°C, for 30–40 minutes, until golden brown and the cheese topping is hot and bubbling. Garnish with fresh basil leaves, if liked, and serve immediately.

VARIATION

Try substituting smoked Bavarian cheese for the mozzarella or halloumi and grated Cheddar cheese for the Parmesan, for a slightly different but equally delicious flavor.

Paglia e Fieno

The name of this dish—"straw and hay"—refers to the colors of the pasta when mixed together.

NUTRITIONAL INFORMATION

Calories	 699	Sugars	.... 7g
Protein	.... 26g	Fat	.... 39g
Carbohydrate	.. 65g	Saturates	..... 23g

10 mins   10 mins

SERVES 4

INGREDIENTS

4 tbsp butter

1 lb/450 g fresh peas, shelled

scant 1 cup heavy cream

1 lb/450 g mixed fresh green and white spaghetti or tagliatelle

1 tbsp olive oil

$^2/_3$ cup freshly grated Parmesan cheese, plus shavings to serve

pinch of freshly grated nutmeg

salt and pepper

1 Melt the butter in a large pan. Add the fresh peas and cook, over a low heat, for 2–3 minutes.

2 Using a measuring cup, pour $^2/_3$ cup of the cream into the pan, bring to a boil, and simmer for 1–1$^1/_2$ minutes, or until the mixture is slightly thickened. Remove the pan from the heat.

3 Meanwhile, bring a large pan of lightly salted water to a boil. Add the spaghetti or tagliatelle and olive oil and cook for 2–3 minutes, or until just tender, but still firm to the bite. Remove the pan from the heat, drain the pasta thoroughly and return to the pan.

4 Add the peas and cream sauce to the pasta. Return the pan to the heat and add the remaining cream and the grated Parmesan cheese, and season to taste with salt, pepper, and grated nutmeg.

5 Using 2 forks, gently toss the pasta to coat with the peas and cream sauce, while heating through.

6 Transfer the pasta to a serving dish and serve immediately, topped with shavings of Parmesan cheese.

VARIATION

Sauté 2 cups sliced white or oyster mushrooms in 4 tbsp butter over a low heat for 4–5 minutes. Stir into the peas and cream sauce just before adding to the pasta in step 4.

Green Tagliatelle with Garlic

A rich pasta dish for garlic lovers everywhere. It is quick and easy to prepare, and full of flavor.

NUTRITIONAL INFORMATION

Calories	526	Sugars	3g
Protein	14g	Fat	34g
Carbohydrate	45g	Saturates	13g

5 mins   20 mins

SERVES 4

INGREDIENTS

2 tbsp walnut oil

1 bunch scallions, sliced

2 garlic cloves, thinly sliced

3¼ cups sliced mushrooms

1 lb/450 g fresh green and white tagliatelle

1 tbsp olive oil

8 oz/225 g frozen spinach, thawed and drained

½ cup full-fat soft cheese with garlic and herbs

4 tbsp light cream

½ cup chopped, unsalted pistachios

2 tbsp shredded fresh basil

TO GARNISH

fresh basil sprigs

Italian bread, to serve

3 Meanwhile, bring a large pan of lightly salted water to the boil. Add the tagliatelle and olive oil and cook for 3–5 minutes, or until tender, but still firm to the bite. Drain the tagliatelle thoroughly and return to the pan.

4 Add the spinach to the skillet and heat through for 1–2 minutes. Add the cheese to the pan and allow to melt slightly. Stir in the cream and continue to cook, without allowing the mixture to come to a boil, until warmed through.

5 Pour the sauce over the pasta, season to taste with salt and black pepper, and mix well. Heat through gently, stirring constantly, for 2–3 minutes.

6 Transfer the pasta to a serving dish and sprinkle with the pistachios and shredded basil. Garnish with the basil sprigs and serve immediately with the Italian bread of your choice.

1 Heat the walnut oil in a large skillet. Add the scallions and garlic and cook for 1 minute, until just softened.

2 Add the mushrooms to the pan, stir well, cover, and cook over a low heat for about 5 minutes, until softened.

Patriotic Pasta

The ingredients of this dish have the same bright colors as the Italian flag—hence its name.

NUTRITIONAL INFORMATION

Calories 325   Sugars 5g
Protein .... 8g   Fat 13g
Carbohydrate .. 48g   Saturates 2g

🥗 5 mins   🕐 15 mins

SERVES 4

INGREDIENTS

1 lb/450 g dried farfalle

4 tbsp olive oil

1 lb/450 g cherry tomatoes

3 oz/90 g arugula

salt and pepper

romano cheese, to garnish

1 Bring a large pan of lightly salted water to a boil. Add the farfalle and 1 tablespoon of the olive oil and cook for 8–10 minutes, or until tender, but still firm to the bite. Drain the farfalle thoroughly and return to the pan.

2 Cut the cherry tomatoes in half and trim the arugula.

3 Heat the remaining olive oil in a large pan. Add the tomatoes to the pan and cook for 1 minute. Add the farfalle and arugula to the pan and stir gently to mix. Heat the mixture through and season to taste with salt and pepper.

4 Meanwhile, using a vegetable peeler, shave thin slices of romano cheese.

5 Transfer the farfalle and vegetables to a warm serving dish. Garnish with the cheese shavings and serve immediately.

COOK'S TIP

Romano cheese is a hard sheep's milk cheese which resembles Parmesan, and is often used for grating over a variety of dishes. It has a sharp flavor and is only used in small quantities.

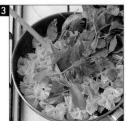

Mediterranean Spaghetti

Delicious Mediterranean vegetables, cooked in rich tomato sauce, make an ideal topping for nutty whole-wheat pasta.

NUTRITIONAL INFORMATION

Calories	547	Sugars	19g
Protein	16g	Fat	16g
Carbohydrate	91g	Saturates	5g

5 mins

35 mins

SERVES 4

INGREDIENTS

2 tbsp olive oil

1 large red onion, chopped

2 garlic cloves, crushed

1 tbsp lemon juice

4 baby eggplants, quartered

2½ cups sieved tomatoes

2 tsp superfine sugar

2 tbsp tomato paste

14 oz/400 g canned artichoke hearts, drained and halved

1 cup pitted black olives

12 oz/350 g dried spaghetti

2 tbsp butter

salt and pepper

fresh basil sprigs, to garnish

olive bread, to serve

1 Heat 1 tablespoon of the olive oil in a large skillet. Add the onion, garlic, lemon juice, and eggplants, and cook over a low heat for 4–5 minutes, until the onion and eggplants are lightly golden brown.

2 Pour in the sieved tomatoes, season to taste, and stir in the superfine sugar and tomato paste. Bring to a boil, then lower the heat and simmer, stirring occasionally, for 20 minutes.

3 Gently stir in the artichoke hearts and black olives and cook for 5 minutes.

4 Meanwhile, bring a large pan of lightly salted water to a boil. Add the spaghetti and remaining oil and cook for 7–8 minutes, or until tender, but still firm to the bite.

5 Drain the spaghetti thoroughly, toss with the butter to coat it well, and transfer to a large serving dish.

6 Pour the vegetable sauce over the spaghetti, garnish with fresh basil sprigs and serve immediately with slices of olive bread.

Spinach & Mushroom Lasagna

This is one of the tastiest vegetarian dishes. For a variation you could substitute sliced roasted bell peppers for the spinach (see below).

NUTRITIONAL INFORMATION

Calories ...... 720 Sugars 9g
Protein .... 31g Fat 52g
Carbohydrate ...36g Saturates 32g

20 mins · 40 mins

SERVES 4

INGREDIENTS

½ cup butter, plus extra for greasing

2 garlic cloves, finely chopped

4 oz/115 g shallots

8 oz/225 g wild mushrooms, such as chanterelles

1 lb/450 g spinach, cooked, drained and finely chopped

2 cups grated Cheddar cheese

¼ tsp freshly grated nutmeg

1 tsp chopped fresh basil

2 oz/60 g all-purpose flour

2½ cups hot milk

⅔ cup grated Cheshire cheese

salt and pepper

8 sheets pre-cooked lasagna

1 Lightly grease a large ovenproof dish with a little butter.

2 Melt half of the butter in a pan. Add the garlic, shallots, and mushrooms, and cook over a low heat for 3 minutes. Stir in the spinach, Cheddar cheese, nutmeg, and basil. Season with salt and pepper to taste and set aside.

3 Melt the remaining butter in another pan over a low heat. Add the flour and cook, stirring constantly, for 1 minute. Gradually stir in the hot milk, whisking constantly until smooth. Stir in ¼ cup of the Cheshire cheese and season to taste with salt and pepper.

4 Spread half of the mushroom and spinach mixture over the bottom of the prepared dish. Cover with a layer of lasagna, then with half of the cheese sauce. Repeat the process and sprinkle over the remaining Cheshire cheese.

5 Bake in a preheated oven, 400°F/200°C, for 30 minutes, or until golden brown. Serve hot.

VARIATION

You could substitute 4 bell peppers for the spinach. Roast in a preheated oven, 400°F/200°C, for 20 minutes. Rub off the skins under cold water, deseed, and chop before using.

Spaghetti & Mushroom Sauce

This easy vegetarian dish is ideal for busy people with little time, but plenty of good taste!

NUTRITIONAL INFORMATION

Calories	604	Sugars	5g
Protein	11g	Fat	39g
Carbohydrate	54g	Saturates	21g

🕒 20 mins   🕐 35 mins

SERVES 4

INGREDIENTS

4 tbsp butter

2 tbsp olive oil

6 shallots, sliced

6 cups sliced white mushrooms

1 tsp all-purpose flour

⅔ cup heavy cream

2 tbsp port

4 oz/115 g sun-dried tomatoes, chopped

freshly grated nutmeg

1 lb/450 g dried spaghetti

1 tbsp freshly chopped parsley

salt and pepper

6 triangles of sautéed white bread, to serve

1 Heat the butter and 1 tablespoon of the oil in a large pan. Add the sliced shallots and cook over a medium heat for 3 minutes. Add the mushrooms and cook over a low heat for 2 minutes. Season with salt and pepper, sprinkle over the flour and cook, stirring constantly, for 1 minute.

2 Gradually stir in the cream and port, add the sun-dried tomatoes and a pinch of grated nutmeg, and cook over a low heat for 8 minutes.

3 Meanwhile, bring a large pan of lightly salted water to a boil. Add the spaghetti and remaining olive oil and cook for 12–14 minutes, or until tender, but still firm to the bite.

4 Drain the spaghetti and return to the pan. Pour over the mushroom sauce and cook for 3 minutes. Transfer the spaghetti to a large serving plate and sprinkle over the chopped parsley. Serve with crispy triangles of sautéed bread.

VARIATION

Non-vegetarians could add 4 oz/115 g prosciutto, cut into thin strips and heated gently in 2 tbsp butter, to the pasta, along with the mushroom sauce.

Walnut & Olive Fettuccine

This mouth-watering dish would make an excellent light, vegetarian lunch for four, or a good appetizer for six.

NUTRITIONAL INFORMATION

Calories 804   Sugars 5g
Protein .... 19g   Fat 65g
Carbohydrate .. 34g   Saturates 15g

10 mins   5 mins

SERVES 4–6

I N G R E D I E N T S

2 thick slices whole-wheat bread,
  crusts removed

1¼ cups milk

2½ cups shelled walnuts

2 garlic cloves, crushed

1 cup pitted black olives

⅔ cup freshly grated Parmesan cheese

½ cup extra virgin olive oil

⅔ cup heavy cream

1 lb/450 g fresh fettuccine

salt and pepper

2–3 tbsp chopped fresh parsley

4 Bring a large pan of lightly salted water to a boil. Add the fettuccine and half of the remaining oil and cook for 2–3 minutes, or until tender, but still firm to the bite. Drain thoroughly, and toss with the remaining olive oil.

5 Divide the cooked fettuccine between individual serving plates, and spoon the olive, garlic, and walnut sauce on top. Sprinkle over the fresh parsley and serve.

1 Put the bread in a shallow dish, pour over the milk and set aside to soak until the liquid has been absorbed.

2 Spread the walnuts out on a cookie sheet and toast in a preheated oven, 375°F/190°C, for about 5 minutes, until golden. Set aside to cool.

3 Put the soaked bread, walnuts, garlic, olives, Parmesan cheese, and 6 tablespoons of the olive oil in a food processor and blend to a paste. Season to taste and stir in the cream.

Pasta & Vegetable Sauce

The shapes and textures of the vegetables make a mouthwatering presentation in this light and summery dish.

NUTRITIONAL INFORMATION

Calories	389	Sugars	4g
Protein	16g	Fat	20g
Carbohydrate	38g	Saturates	11g

10 mins　　30 mins

SERVES 4

INGREDIENTS

8 oz/225 g dried gemelli or other pasta shapes

1 tbsp olive oil

1 head green broccoli, cut into florets

2 zucchini, sliced

8 oz/225 g asparagus spears

4 oz/115 g snow peas

4 oz/115 g frozen peas

2 tbsp butter

3 tbsp vegetable bouillon

4 tbsp heavy cream

freshly grated nutmeg

2 tbsp chopped fresh parsley

2 tbsp freshly grated Parmesan cheese

salt and pepper

1 Bring a large pan of lightly salted water to a boil. Add the pasta and olive oil and cook for 8–10 minutes, or until tender, but still firm to the bite. Drain, return to the pan, cover and keep warm.

2 Steam the broccoli, zucchini, asparagus spears, and snow peas over a pan of boiling salted water until they are just beginning to soften, then remove from the heat and refresh in cold water. Drain and set aside.

3 Bring a small pan of lightly salted water to a boil. Add the frozen peas and cook for 3 minutes. Drain the peas, refresh in cold water, then drain again. Set aside with the other vegetables.

4 Put the butter and vegetable bouillon in a pan over a medium heat. Add all of the vegetables, reserving a few of the asparagus spears, and toss carefully with a wooden spoon until they have heated through, taking care not to break them up.

5 Stir in the cream and heat through without bringing to a boil. Season to taste with salt, pepper, and nutmeg.

6 Transfer the pasta to a warmed serving dish and stir in the chopped parsley. Spoon over the vegetable sauce and sprinkle over the Parmesan cheese. Arrange the reserved asparagus spears in a pattern on top and serve.

Filled Eggplants

Combined with tomatoes and melting mozzarella cheese, pasta makes a tasty filling for baked eggplant shells.

NUTRITIONAL INFORMATION

Calories	342	Sugars	6g
Protein	11g	Fat	16g
Carbohydrate	40g	Saturates	4g

25 mins　　55 mins

SERVES 4

INGREDIENTS

8 oz/225 g dried penne or other short pasta shapes

4 tbsp olive oil, plus extra for brushing

2 eggplants

1 large onion, chopped

2 garlic cloves, crushed

14 oz/400 g canned chopped tomatoes

2 tsp dried oregano

2 oz/55 g mozzarella cheese, thinly sliced

¼ cup freshly grated Parmesan cheese

2 tbsp dry breadcrumbs

salt and pepper

salad greens, to serve

1 Bring a large pan of lightly salted water to a boil. Add the pasta and 1 tablespoon of the olive oil, bring back to a boil and then cook for 8–10 minutes, or until tender, but firm to the bite. Drain, return to the pan, cover and keep warm.

2 Cut the eggplants in half lengthwise and score around the inside with a sharp knife, being careful not to pierce the shells. Scoop out the flesh with a spoon. Brush the insides of the shells with olive oil. Chop the flesh and set aside.

3 Heat the remaining oil in a skillet. Cook the onion until translucent. Add the garlic and cook for 1 minute, then add the chopped eggplant and cook, stirring frequently, for 5 minutes.

4 Add the chopped tomatoes and oregano, and season to taste with salt and pepper. Bring the mixture to a boil and simmer for 10 minutes, or until thickened. Remove from the heat and stir in the pasta.

5 Brush a cookie sheet with oil and arrange the eggplant shells in a single layer. Divide half of the tomato and pasta mixture between them. Scatter over the mozzarella slices, then pile the remaining tomato and pasta mixture on top. Mix the Parmesan and breadcrumbs and sprinkle over, pressing it lightly into the mixture.

6 Bake in a preheated oven, 400°F/ 200°C, for about 25 minutes, or until the topping is golden brown. Serve hot with a selection of mixed salad greens.

Lemon-Flavored Spaghetti

Steaming vegetables helps to preserve their nutritional content and allows them to retain their bright, natural colors and crunchy texture.

NUTRITIONAL INFORMATION

Calories	133	Sugars	8g
Protein	8g	Fat	1g
Carbohydrate	25g	Saturates	0.2g

🕒 10 mins   🕐 25 mins

SERVES 4

INGREDIENTS

8 oz/225 g celery root

2 medium carrots

2 medium leeks

1 small red bell pepper

1 small yellow bell pepper

2 garlic cloves

1 tsp celery seeds

1 tbsp lemon juice

10½ oz/300 g spaghetti

chopped celery leaves, to garnish

LEMON DRESSING

1 tsp finely grated lemon zest

1 tbsp lemon juice

4 tbsp low-fat unsweetened yogurt

salt and pepper

2 tbsp snipped fresh chives

1 Peel the celery root and carrots, cut into very thin sticks and place in a bowl. Trim and slice the leeks, rinse under running water to flush out any trapped dirt, then shred finely. Halve, deseed, and slice the bell peppers. Peel and thinly slice the garlic.

2 Add all of the vegetables to the bowl with the celery root and the carrots. Toss the vegetables with the celery seeds and lemon juice.

3 Bring a large pan of water to a boil and cook the spaghetti according to the instructions on the packet. Drain and keep warm.

4 Meanwhile, bring another large pan of water to a boil, put the vegetables in a steamer or strainer and place over the boiling water. Cover and steam for 6–7 minutes, or until the vegetables are just tender.

5 While the spaghetti and vegetables are cooking, mix the ingredients for the lemon dressing together.

6 Transfer the spaghetti and vegetables to a warm serving bowl and mix with the dressing. Garnish with chopped celery leaves and serve.

Pesto Pasta

Italian pesto is usually laden with fat. This version has just as much flavor but is much healthier.

NUTRITIONAL INFORMATION

Calories	283	Sugars	5g
Protein	14g	Fat	3g
Carbohydrate	37g	Saturates	1g

1 hr   30 mins

SERVES 4

INGREDIENTS

8 oz/225 g crimini mushrooms, sliced

¾ cup fresh vegetable bouillon

6 oz/175 g asparagus, trimmed and cut into 2 inch/5 cm lengths

10½ oz/300 g green and white tagliatelle

14 oz/400 g canned artichoke hearts, drained and halved

grissini (bread sticks), to serve

PESTO SAUCE

2 large garlic cloves, crushed

½ oz/15 g fresh basil leaves, washed

6 tbsp low-fat unsweetened yogurt

2 tbsp freshly grated Parmesan cheese

salt and pepper

TO GARNISH

shredded fresh basil leaves

Parmesan cheese shavings

1 Place the mushrooms in a pan with the bouillon. Bring to a boil, cover, and simmer for 3–4 minutes until just tender. Drain and set aside, reserving the liquor to use in soups if wished.

2 Bring a small pan of water to a boil and cook the asparagus for 3–4 minutes until just tender. Drain and set aside until required.

3 Bring a large pan of lightly salted water to a boil and cook the tagliatelle according to the instructions on the packet. Drain, return to the pan, and keep warm.

4 Meanwhile, make the pesto. Place all of the ingredients in a blender or food processor and process for a few seconds until smooth. Alternatively, finely chop the basil and mix all the ingredients together.

5 Add the mushrooms, asparagus, and artichoke hearts to the pasta and cook, stirring, over a low heat for 2–3 minutes.

6 Remove the pasta and vegetable mixture from the heat and stir in the pesto. Stir well to mix.

7 Transfer to a warm bowl. Garnish with shredded basil leaves and Parmesan shavings and serve with grissini.

Pasta & Herring Salad

This salad, which so many countries claim as their own, is considered in Holland to be a typically Dutch dish.

NUTRITIONAL INFORMATION

Calories	774	Sugars	.......21g
Protein	.......33g	Fat	..........31g
Carbohydrate	..97g	Saturates	......4g

1½ hrs   15 mins

SERVES 4

INGREDIENTS

9 oz/250 g dried pasta shells

5 tbsp olive oil

14 oz/400 g rollmop herrings in brine

6 boiled potatoes

2 large tart apples

2 baby frisée lettuces

2 baby beets

4 hard-cooked eggs

6 pickled onions

6 dill pickles

2 tbsp capers

3 tbsp of tarragon vinegar

salt and pepper

1 Bring a large pan of lightly salted water to a boil. Add the pasta and 1 tablespoon of the olive oil and cook until tender, but still firm to the bite. Drain the pasta thoroughly and refresh in cold water.

2 Cut the herrings, potatoes, apples, frisée lettuces, and beets into small pieces. Put all of these ingredients into a large salad bowl.

3 Drain the pasta thoroughly and add to the salad bowl. Toss lightly to mix the pasta and herring mixture together. Season.

4 Carefully shell the hard-cooked eggs, then slice them. Garnish the salad with the slices of egg, pickled onions, dill pickles, and capers, sprinkle with the remaining olive oil and the tarragon vinegar, and season to taste. Serve immediately.

VARIATION

This recipe also works well with whole-wheat pasta, which complements the richness of the fish.

Cheese, Nut & Pasta Salad

Use colorful salad greens to provide visual contrast to match the contrasts of taste and texture.

NUTRITIONAL INFORMATION

Calories	694	Sugars	1g
Protein	22g	Fat	57g
Carbohydrate	24g	Saturates	15g

15 mins   15–20 mins

SERVES 4

INGREDIENTS

8 oz/225 g dried pasta shells

1 tbsp olive oil

1 cup shelled and halved walnuts

mixed salad greens, such as radicchio, escarole, arugula, corn salad, and frisée

8 oz/225 g dolcelatte cheese, crumbled

salt

DRESSING

2 tbsp walnut oil

4 tbsp extra virgin olive oil

2 tbsp red wine vinegar

salt and pepper

1 Bring a large pan of lightly salted water to a boil. Add the pasta shells and olive oil and cook for 8–10 minutes, or until tender, but still firm to the bite. Drain the pasta, refresh under cold running water, drain thoroughly again, and set aside.

2 Spread out the shelled walnut halves on to a cookie sheet and toast under a preheated broiler for 2–3 minutes. Set aside to cool while you make the dressing.

3 To make the dressing, whisk together the walnut oil, olive oil, and vinegar in a small bowl, and season to taste.

4 To make up the salad, arrange the salad greens in a large serving bowl. Pile the cooled pasta in the middle of the salad greens and sprinkle over the dolcelatte cheese. Just before serving, pour the dressing over the pasta salad, scatter over the walnut halves, and toss together to mix and to coat in the dressing. Serve immediately.

COOK'S TIP

Dolcelatte is a semi-soft, blue-veined cheese from Italy. Its texture is creamy and smooth and the flavor is delicate, but piquant. You could use Roquefort instead. It is essential that whatever cheese you choose, it is of the best quality and in peak condition.

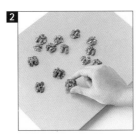

Goat Cheese & Penne Salad

This superb salad is delicious when served with strongly flavored meat dishes, such as venison.

NUTRITIONAL INFORMATION

Calories	634	Sugars	13g
Protein	18g	Fat	51g
Carbohydrate	27g	Saturates	13g

1 hr 5 mins   10 mins

SERVES 4

INGREDIENTS

9 oz/250 g dried penne

5 tbsp olive oil

1 head radicchio, torn into pieces

1 Webbs lettuce, torn into pieces

generous ½ cup chopped walnuts

2 ripe pears, cored and diced

1 fresh basil sprig

4 oz/115 g young spinach leaves, coarsely chopped, or watercress, trimmed

2 tbsp lemon juice

3 tbsp garlic vinegar

4 tomatoes, quartered

1 small onion, sliced

1 large carrot, grated

9 oz/250 g goat cheese, diced

salt and pepper

COOK'S TIP

Radicchio is a variety of endive which originated in Italy. It has a slightly bitter flavor.

1 Bring a large pan of lightly salted water to a boil. Add the penne and 1 tablespoon of the olive oil and cook for 8–10 minutes, or until tender, but still firm to the bite. Drain the pasta, refresh under cold running water, drain thoroughly again, and set aside to cool.

2 Place the radicchio and Webbs lettuce in a large salad bowl and mix together well. Top with the pasta, walnuts, pears, basil, and spinach or watercress.

3 Mix together the lemon juice, the remaining olive oil, and the vinegar in a measuring cup. Pour the mixture over the salad ingredients and toss to coat the salad greens well.

4 Add the tomato quarters, onion slices, grated carrot, and diced goat cheese to the salad, and toss together using 2 forks until well mixed. Let the finished salad chill in the refrigerator for about 1 hour before serving.

Pasta & Garlic Mayo Salad

This crisp salad would make an excellent accompaniment to broiled meat and is ideal for summer barbecue grills.

NUTRITIONAL INFORMATION

Calories 858	Sugars 35g	
Protein 11g	Fat 64g	
Carbohydrate .. 64g	Saturates 8g	

🥄 1½ hours   🕐 10 mins

SERVES 4

INGREDIENTS

2 large lettuces

9 oz/250 g dried penne

1 tbsp olive oil

8 red eating apples

juice of 4 lemons

1 bunch of celery stalks, sliced

¾ cup shelled, halved walnuts

1⅛ cups fresh garlic mayonnaise
   (see Cook's Tip)

salt

1 Wash, drain, and dry the lettuce leaves with paper towels. Transfer them to the refrigerator for 1 hour or until crisp.

2 Meanwhile, bring a large pan of lightly salted water to a boil. Add the pasta and olive oil and cook for 8–10 minutes, or until tender, but still firm to the bite. Drain the pasta and refresh under cold running water. Drain again and set aside.

3 Core and dice the apples, place them in a bowl, and sprinkle with lemon juice.

4 Mix together the pasta, celery, apples, and walnuts, and toss in the garlic mayonnaise (see Cook's Tip, below).

5 Line a salad bowl with the lettuce leaves and spoon the pasta salad into the lined bowl before serving.

COOK'S TIP

For garlic mayo, beat 2 egg yolks with a pinch of salt and 6 crushed garlic cloves. Beat in 12 fl oz/ 350 ml oil, 1–2 teaspoons at a time. When ¼ of the oil has been incorporated, beat in 1–2 tablespoons white wine vinegar. Continue beating in the oil. Stir in 1 teaspoon Dijon mustard and season.

Italian Fusilli Salad

Tomatoes and mozzarella cheese are a classic Italian combination. Here they are joined with pasta spirals and avocado for a touch of luxury.

NUTRITIONAL INFORMATION

Calories 660	Sugars 7g	
Protein 22g	Fat 47g	
Carbohydrate .. 39g	Saturates 13g	

15 mins   10 mins

SERVES 4

INGREDIENTS

2 tbsp pine nuts

6 oz/175 g dried fusilli

1 tbsp olive oil

6 tomatoes

8 oz/225 g mozzarella cheese

1 large avocado pear

2 tbsp lemon juice

3 tbsp chopped fresh basil

salt and pepper

fresh basil sprigs, to garnish

DRESSING

6 tbsp extra virgin olive oil

2 tbsp white wine vinegar

1 tsp whole-grain mustard

pinch of sugar

1 Spread the pine nuts out on a cookie sheet and toast under a preheated broiler for 1–2 minutes until golden. Remove and set aside to cool.

2 Bring a large pan of lightly salted water to a boil. Add the fusilli and olive oil and cook until tender, but still firm to the bite. Drain the pasta thoroughly and refresh in cold water. Drain again and set aside to cool.

3 Thinly slice the tomatoes and the mozzarella cheese.

4 Cut the avocado pear in half and remove the pit and skin. Cut into thin slices lengthwise and sprinkle with lemon juice to prevent discoloration.

5 To make the dressing, whisk together the oil, vinegar, mustard, and sugar in a small bowl, and season to taste with salt and black pepper.

6 Arrange the tomato, mozzarella, and avocado slices alternately, overlapping one another, on a large serving platter.

7 Toss the cooled pasta with half of the dressing and the chopped basil, and season to taste with salt and black pepper. Spoon the pasta into the center of the serving platter and pour over the remaining dressing. Sprinkle the toasted pine nuts, over the pasta, garnish with fresh basil sprigs, and serve immediately.

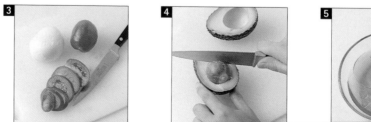

Spicy Sausage Salad

A warm sausage and pasta dressing spooned over chilled salad greens makes a refreshing combination to start a meal.

NUTRITIONAL INFORMATION

Calories 383   Sugars 2g
Protein .... 11g   Fat 28g
Carbohydrate .. 20g   Saturates 1g

15 mins   25 mins

SERVES 4

I N G R E D I E N T S

4½ oz/125 g small pasta shapes, such as elbow tubetti

3 tbsp olive oil

1 medium onion, chopped

2 cloves garlic, crushed

1 small yellow bell pepper, cored, deseeded, and cut into very thin sticks

6 oz/175 g spicy pork sausage such as chorizo, Italian pepperoni or salami, skinned and sliced

2 tbsp red wine

1 tbsp red wine vinegar

mixed salad greens, chilled

salt

1 Cook the pasta in a pan of boiling salted water, adding 1 tablespoon of the oil, for 8–10 minutes, or until tender. Drain and set aside.

2 Heat the remaining oil in a pan over a medium heat. Cook the onion until it is translucent, stir in the garlic, yellow bell pepper, and sliced sausage, and cook for 3–4 minutes, stirring once or twice.

3 Add the wine, wine vinegar, and reserved pasta to the pan, stir to blend well, and bring the mixture just to a boil.

4 Arrange the chilled salad greens on individual serving plates, spoon on the warm sausage and pasta mixture, and serve immediately.

VARIATION

Other suitable sausages include the Italian pepperoni, flavored with chile peppers, fennel, and spices, and one of the many varieties of salami, usually flavored with garlic and pepper.

This is a Parragon Publishing Book
This edition published in 2003

Parragon Publishing
Queen Street House
4 Queen Street
Bath BA1 1HE, UK

ISBN: 1-40540-878-2

Printed in China

NOTE

This book uses metric and imperial measurements. Follow the same units
of measurement throughout; do not mix metric and imperial.
All spoon measurements are level: teaspoons are assumed to be 5 ml, and
tablespoons are assumed to be 15 ml. Unless otherwise stated,
milk is assumed to be full fat, eggs and individual vegetables such as potatoes
are medium, and pepper is freshly ground black pepper.

The nutritional information provided for each recipe is per serving or per person.
Optional ingredients, variations or serving suggestions have
not been included in the calculations. The times given for each recipe are an approximate
guide only because the preparation times may differ according to the techniques used by
different people and the cooking times may vary as a result of the type of oven used.

Recipes using raw or very lightly cooked eggs should be
avoided by infants, the elderly, pregnant women, convalescents,
and anyone suffering from an illness.

The publisher would like to thank
Steamer Trading Cookshop, Lewes, East Sussex, for the kind loan of props.